SHRUB IT UP

BY GEORGE MCNAIR

Publishing	CGM Publishing P.O. Box 1107, Bandon, Oregon
Editing	Chris McNair Sharon Wilson
Word Processing by:	Susan Hyne Etc. Enterprises Medford, Oregon
Cover:	Don Tippit Sign Painter/Graphic Artist Grants Pass, Oregon
Graphics:	George McNair
...ting:	The News Press Printing Company Coos Bay, Oregon

-0-6

About the Author

The elusive trade secrets contained within this guide were discovered from on the ground experience while working with other professionals and from the University of Oregon where I graduated with a Bachelor of Landscape Architecture in 1973. The term "Shrub It Up" was coined by a friend at school who would say, "Shrub It Up" right before we would begin another design project.

My experiences as Jackson County park planner, Forest Service landscape architect, and landscape contractor have provided valuable insight for the "nuts and bolts" operations of building a landscape. It all seems simple until one tries, then reality sets in. Usually the first time through, people waste time and money trying to improve the looks of their property and the whole effort can be disappointing when finished. Even for years later, because the same look keeps growing either better or worse. This guide was written to enable people to improve their home or business setting through landscaping with good success; even the first time through!

When I first began working as a landscape architect, it was with the Forest Service then later I went to work for the original landscape architect in Medford, Dale Coverstone. Dale has been practicing for over twenty four years and provides landscape plans for a variety of commercial and residential projects. The "nuts and bolts" of landscaping were learned from Bruce Bateman, the original landscape contractor in the Medford area and past president of the Oregon Board of Landscape contractors. The two people mentioned provided valuable insight that serves as the foundation for this landscape book.

Neat, lush green landscapes makes our sometimes wire infested, bleak cities more liv able and attractive for new business but many times the landscaping is seen as a frill to be cut when the budget is tight. This makes as much sense as getting a "crew" cut because it is too expensive to go to the barber or hair dresser. If you have the chance, observe the landscaping of the world's greatest computer companies in the "Silicon Valley" where landscaping took a top priority. The first impression is important for people, homes and business. Well, that's enough on landscaping. This guide will be valuable for creating a good landscape and hopefully it will have a part in many landscapes throughout the Pacific Northwest.

Book Reviews

"This basic landscaping guide for the home gardener contains a good deal of useful information in an easy to use form."
 - Miles McCoy, editor for the Oregon Association
   of Nurserymen, Inc.

"Shrub It Up is easy to understand, technically sound, and humorously presented. A must for the homeowner and a valuable reference guide for the landscape professional."
 - Bruce Bateman, President of the Oregon Board
   Landscape Contractors. (1975 - 1980)

"Shrub It Up provides easily understood guidelines and quick answers ... a useful take home reference."
 - George Tiger, Oregon State University Extension Agent

"George McNair's graphics and ability to teach, which comes through, are worth double the price of the book ... alone."
 - Steve Potter, Landscape Architect, Medford, Oregon

"The book gives you practical, informative, detailed advice on how to plan the landscaping of your property so that it will look good when all the trees and shrubs have reached full size."
 - Cleve Twitchell of the Medford Mail Tribune Newspaper

FOREWORD

Many times people find themselves with a new home, or office, a bare ground landscape and a limited budget. They decide to landscape the bare ground with the intent of creating one of the most original creations ever invented. After a few days of feverish labor and absolute confusion in the nursery, the whole project begins to turn into a monster that quickly devours their budget and then turns on them. Would you like a neat, appealing landscape for the home or office that avoids the budget monster and will appreciate in value with age?

This basic landscape design and construction guide was written to help people avoid the jaws of the monster. This guide can be read in one afternoon by the eager landscaper and provides a person with the carefully guarded tricks of the landscape trade. It will help a person at least get in the ballpark, then with a little research and ideas from consultants, a top landscape can be achieved. This guide will also help clear up confusion in the nursery, where most landscape crimes begin, like when a person buys a cute little bush for a 2'x2' planter that will eventually grow into a huge 20' wide, ugly prickly bush. This guide contains charts that give the scoop on plants such as where they like to grow, what they look like and how big they get. The plants listed in this guide will grow in the temperate regions of Oregon, Washington and Northern California that are zones 4, 5, 6 and 7. Zones are regions designated by the nursery industry that vary in climate. For example, Seattle, Washington is zone 5, the Willamette Valley is zone 6 and the Rogue Valley is zone 7. Nurseries stock plants that do well in your area, so use this guide to prepare a plant list, then go out to a nursery and find the plants or allow the nursery to substitute similar plants.

A good landscape, like a good wine, improves with age and will greatly add to the property value. Some people think landscaping is a "waste of money," so they spend every last dime on a neat building that will sit in the middle of a zero landscape. This is like buying a Picasso painting and framing it with mat board and "saran wrap." A typical landscape will average 5% to 10% of the typical home price, so set enough money aside for landscaping. Treat your investment right! Two one-gallon shrubs saved by this guide will pay for it! The plants listed pertain to your area only and are the most commonly used plants, with some exotics included.

This manual was planned to be to-the-point and basic, so readers can comprehend the elemental landscape design and construction principles. Some people with technical problems will need to supplement this manual with research from professional consultants, while others will dig right in. Good landscaping!

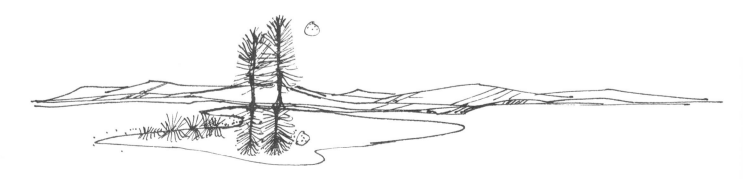

Table of Contents

chapter 1
LANDSCAPE DESIGN

Thinking through your landscape plan should be done, even if you are in a big hurry to turn your property into the eighth wonder of the world. Most people who do not plan, wonder why they did what they did eight years later, when the giant sequoia begins to uproot the house, the lawn looks like an abstract painting with greens and yellows or the cute little shrubs have turned into little monsters that are covering the windows, walks and lawn. This may seem ridiculously funny but it happens every day when people begin digging and planting without forming good plans. So slow down, plan, then work and enjoy a landscape that will grow more beautiful every year with a minimum of pruning, weeding, watering effort and lawn mowing. A plan will enable you to predict cost, work out the simplest solutions, design irrigation, and will help you create a logical work sequence that is very important with landscape construction. For example, many people have fences built, then find out they need top soil when the access for a dump truck is blocked, so they either tear part of the fence out or wheelbarrow the dirt in. Plan first and work later.

Plan ahead first, then begin the work!!

Locate Property Lines

Before getting carried away, locate your property corner pins and easements for driveways and buried utility lines. Overlooking this step can cause big problems later on as when your rose garden lies on top of the city's utility easement and they need to dig it up with a backhoe! This information is available in the county assessor's office. Obtain a xerox copy of the property like the survey plan shown on this page. Get a 100-foot tape measure, measure off distances and estimate the angles; then scrape the weeds and surface soil off with a shovel until a metal corner pin is found. A metal detector works great for this. If this fails, hire a surveyor to do the job. Remember, new neighbors may locate the exact property lines and insist that your new fence be moved even if it is a foot off.

SEC. 22 TWP. 37 S. R.1 W. W.M.

SCALE 1"= 100'

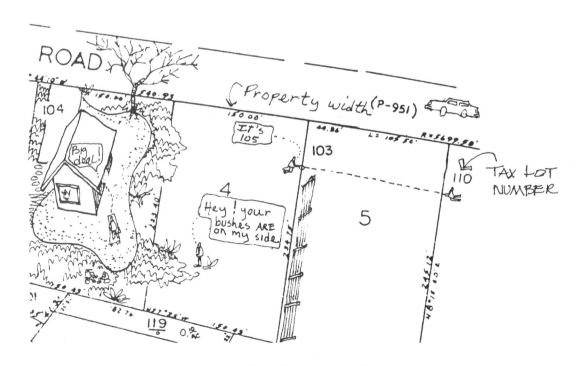

Locate your property lines before doing any landscaping.

Utility Lines

The greatest landscape plan can be ruined when an electric trunk line is discovered after a steep bank is halfway excavated for a lawn and retaining wall. The trunk line could always be moved for $2,000.00 or the lawn could be cut from 25 to 15' wide, but now plans and contracts need to be revised. Most important of all, people can die from an oversight such as this, so have all lines located first.

Some areas have locating services such as the Rogue Basin Utility Coordinating Council in Medford, Oregon. They spray paint on the ground surface where buried lines such as electric, gas, TV, water and telephone lines are located. This is a free service that depends on donations. Be there when they arrive, so you will understand what color corresponds to what line and how deep the lines are. Each utility company sends a location crew during the same day. Remember, digging through your cable TV line while planting a tree can add a few hundred dollars to your landscape cost, if the line can't be spliced. Cutting an electric line can really brighten up your day!

Have utility companies locate buried lines before digging or it may be a shocker!

Master Plan

Before launching off into digging, raking, rolling and shrub planting, it would be wise to devise a clever landscape plan now. There are various ways to come up with a plan. You can hire a nursery landscape designer, landscape architect, or landscape contractor to provide sketch plans or detail plans that can range in cost from $100 to $1,500.

If you are on a tight budget, can inspire your basic engineering traits and want to draw your own plans, then get a 100' tape, a 24" x 36" piece of plywood, 24" x 36" sheet of vellum tracing paper, pencil, ruler and a triangle. Vellum tracing paper is available in drafting supply stores and comes with 1/8" grid lines that really help with the measuring process. Tape the paper on the board, pick a sunny day and start measuring the house and transfer the measurements to the paper at 1' on the ground to $\frac{1}{4}$" on the paper. Put the house in the middle of the paper and measure out from the house to the property lines, trees, utility lines, rocks, etc. and locate all important features accurately on this base map. Use the triangle for right angles. Tie a weight to the end of the tape so it will stay put when pulled tight; otherwise two of you will be measuring, getting a good spring sunburn and suffering from engineer's confusion.

Locate subsurface rock by checking the local area for rock outcroppings and see if a rock ridge leads to your property. Dig a 3' deep test hole with a post hole digger if you suspect bedrock. Bedrock one foot under the surface can really slow down a tree planting operation. Locate the suspected rock areas on the base map.

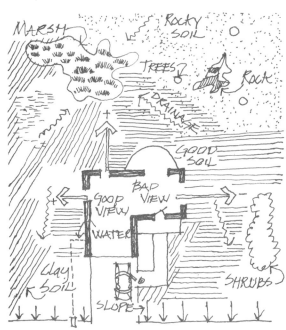

Step 2: Recopy the base map to an accurate scale.

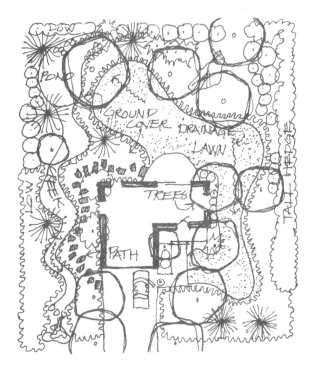

Step 3: Overlay the base map with tracing paper and design away!

Step 1: Prepare a base map that shows all existing features.

Now this base map can be overlaid with another sheet of vellum tracing paper for the final design of the eighth wonder of the world. If the first design turns out like the 800th wonder of the world, here are fourteen general design guidelines:

1. Remember where utility lines are when designing.
2. Show deciduous trees on the south side of the house for summer shade and winter sun; use tall evergreens to block storm winds and bad views.

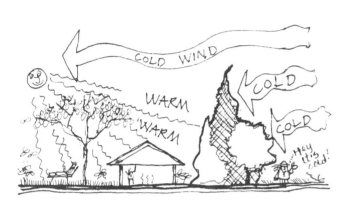

Use plants for a practical purpose.

3. When labeling plants on the plan, refer to the plant list for mature plant sizes and where they like to grow. Some well water contains certain elements, like Boron, that severely stunt plant growth. Ask neighbors if this element is in the water. The county extension agent has a list of plants that will adapt to Boron.
4. Create nice landscape scenes to be seen from windows and block bad views with pine and tall shrubs.
5. Use tall shrubs for backgrounds and work down to short ones in the front. Use combinations of leaf colors, textures, and flower color. A blue house, maroon trees and turquoise junipers may be a little loud. Your reward for all your landscape efforts will be sneers from the neighbors and the "believe it or not" TV crew.
6. Avoid "hodgepodge" landscapes where there is one of everything that looks cute, including pink flamingos, dwarfs, and giant toads. If that's your thing and you want a scientific arboretum, then OK. Otherwise, follow the rule of

repetition and repeat basic plants, then add some of the cute little accent plants to focus on. Repetition creates the harmony and peace; accent plants prevent boredom. This is why a walk in the forest is so calming.

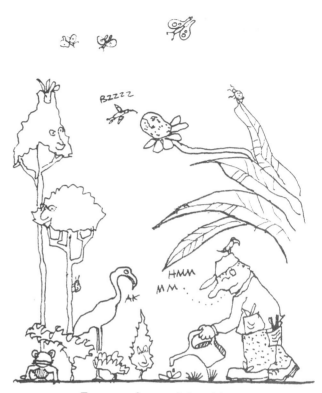

Beware of over doing it!

7. Try to fill in bare ground with ground cover, so the weeds will eventually be choked out.
8. Use the "dominant open space" design principle, where the front is enclosed and mysterious, while a small lawn leads along the side with dense vegetation, ponds, trickling waterfalls and calling birds. The path continues before the back opens into a paradise with a vast expanse of lawn, surrounded with tall background shrubs, flowering trees, and vibrant flowering plants and vines. This principle is advocated by the eminent landscape architect, Mac Ruff, who was dean of the landscape architecture school at the University of Oregon. The dominant open space is easy to mow and cutting other lawn areas down reduces mowing time on Saturday so you can watch the football game or take the kids fishing.

Reduce lawn areas but create a dominant open space.

10. Drain boggy areas with ditches or buried drain pipes unless you want a lawn rice paddy, underwater shrubs, and dead trees. Designing mounds helps keep plants high and dry. Use nature's forms for a fitting landscape or shape the land to drain away from buildings and into drain ditches. Water can be drained into landscaped collection ponds or curving, rocky creeks that are more sightly than straight drain ditches. When the pond fills, the water may drain through buried drain pipes or along the curving, rock creeks. Sump pumps can be used in the pond if the water will not gravity drain. The ponds and creeks should be lined with exposed aggregate cement so leaves and debris can be cleaned out, and the edge can be landscaped with large rocks, ground covers and pines.

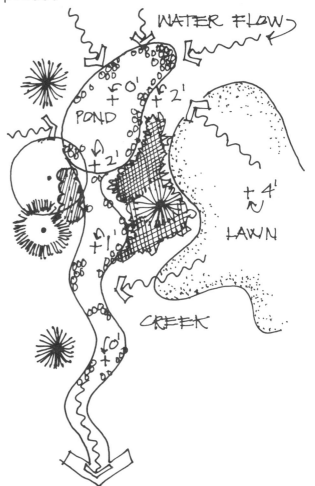

Drainage can be solved with some imagination!

9. In the case of large hillsides or rocky barren areas, consider a natural landscape rather than redoing the site into a typical bark and shrub landscape. It is cheaper to work with nature! Eradicate the hillside weeds, install irrigation, and plant a legume like White Dutch Clover that will provide a nice lush green cover. The clover comes in seed form and is available in some feed and farm supply stores. Along with the clover, plant pine trees and a few shade trees. For rocky barren areas, create a rock garden with drip irrigation, pine trees, patches of ground cover and different sizes, shapes, and colors of rock pebbles.

11. If you are a new home owner, builder, or realtor, and are on a limited budget, then consider a minimum landscape the first year. Plan to add features each year until completed. A minimum landscape is one that provides for site grading, drainage, weed control, shade trees, and some form of irrigation. After grading, plant lots of tall trees, install drip irrigation, apply caseron weed control, cover the site with three inches of fine bark, then apply one inch of coarse bark. Use natural rocks from the site for accent purposes. As time goes by, stake out the future lawn, scrape off the bark, prepare the soil, install spray irrigation, and plant the lawn. Add background shrubs and extend the drip irrigation to supply the shrub beds. This method makes a neat, appealing, inexpensive landscape that features trees, yet is flexible so features can be added later. This type of landscape is initially simple to maintain with the bark and trees, then more features may be added by the owner as funds become available.

12. Plan an automatic underground irrigation system, so your green creation will grow without enslaving you during the summer. Once the plants are in and the hot weather is on, the watering cycle begins, and most people don't have time to set sprinklers for a half hour before the work day begins. This is just one more thing to do or to forget along with remembering if the stove was turned off.

Install the timer operated sprinkler system first, then complete the planting later when you have time. This way, what ever is planted will be watered without added worry. What, it costs too much. If you design your own system and install one yard section at a time, then the costs includes your labor, minus health spa costs since installing irrigation is exercise! Other fixed costs includes pipes, fittings, heads, wire, and a timer. This investment may equal $300, that will in return speed up the appreciation of the home's value since the landscape will now grow effortlessly that adds to the home's marketable charm. The investment is deductable from income in the case of a second home and from capital gains in the case of a main residence. This makes a good mix of green landscaping and green money!

13. Keep it simple is a good rule of thumb, especially if you are new at landscaping. Trying to do too much the first time may permanently squelch your desire for planting again. There is enough to the basics of yard fixing to keep the "professional do it yourselfers" guessing, let alone the beginner. The basics include land shaping, soil preparation, irrigaton, lawns, ground cover, shrubs, and trees. Some bored gardeners like to create challenges by throwing in fountains, night lights, concrete paths, trellises, Egyptian obelisks, Greek sculpture, and Gothic gazeboes, but lets not over do it! Keep it simple and stick with the basics the first time around.

14. Hire a professional consultant for a few hours to check your design and the property. The consultant's ideas may be more practical when it comes to the construction of the rainforest on the arid landscape. A few dollars spent here may prevent lots of misery out in the yard. The seasoned consultants have already made and paid for their past mistakes. The same ones that you will likely make. These pit falls can easily be spotted lurking in your plans by the professional.

Now that we have covered some basic design rules and concepts, it is time to begin laying out the master plan by overlaying the base map with tracing paper, so gather all of the required drafting tools. The idea is to blend the features that you want into one neat design so they fit the land, meet your family's needs, and won't conflict with each other. For example, a play area next to the patio and den, may interrupt adult conversation, and cause the short tempered to yell, so think of these connections. Here are some of the puzzle pieces that need to be fitted in the right spot and are described in this guide: lawns, surface run off, shrub beds, hedges, tree cover, irrigation, rain drainage ponds, drainage creeks, drainage pipes, and mounds.To provide descriptive justice for the following items, this guide would need to be eight hundred pages, so I covered the typical, fundamental landscape elements in detail. The following items are more puzzle pieces that various Sunset and Ortho books cover in detail: walks, patios, decks, hot tubs, fences, play areas, pools, wood storage sheds, garbage, tool sheds, and boat and RV storage. If you are going to have all of these items then you have established one mammoth design problem, and you will need to have an expert mammoth slayer help along the way.

Again, overlay the base map with tracing paper and sketch these special areas on the plan to see how they fit together. Architects call this important design step 'bubble diagraming'. Try several different plans, then pick the one that seems to work. For example, as seen to the right, the small easy to mow lawn was located on the best soil and connects to the patio. The lawn slopes to the drainage pond that fills up like a lake in the winter and looks neat with river rock in the bottom and shrubs all around. The pond overflows and carries the water down the landscaped creek to the storm drain. The rock garden is placed on the poor rocky soil that will suit plants like Rock Cottoneaster, Heath, Rosemary, and other hardy plants. The bad views to the right are screened with hedges while the good views of mountains are left open which is common sense but can easily be overlooked. The hot, right side or south side of the house is shaded with deciduous trees, and the cars are shaded too, so they won't heat up to the point of melting the dashboards! The cool, north side is all ground cover, ferns, and rhododendrons that creates a neat forest scene with the creek, path, and evergreen trees. The ground cover reduces the lawn mowing job, and the evergreen trees block easterly storm winds. As you can see, landscapes have rhyme and reason, or to put it in architectural terms, form and function are essential to good design. Keep designing until the best solution comes around.

Drainage

Summer slowly passes and the land begins to cool off as the glowing sun drifts to the south only to leave the rain clouds in its place. Each day the clouds become a little bolder and threaten to cover the lands with water they collected far out to sea. (We're trying some of Hemmingway's style just for fun! Now back to reality.) As the hot summer slowly passes, the showers begin, and the green lawn gradually fills up like a lake to the point where neighbors think that you are raising carp in among snags that used to be living shrubs. The kids play on the soggy lawn, and it turns into a mud hole, then later the mud gets tracked all over the floors. This sounds horrible, but

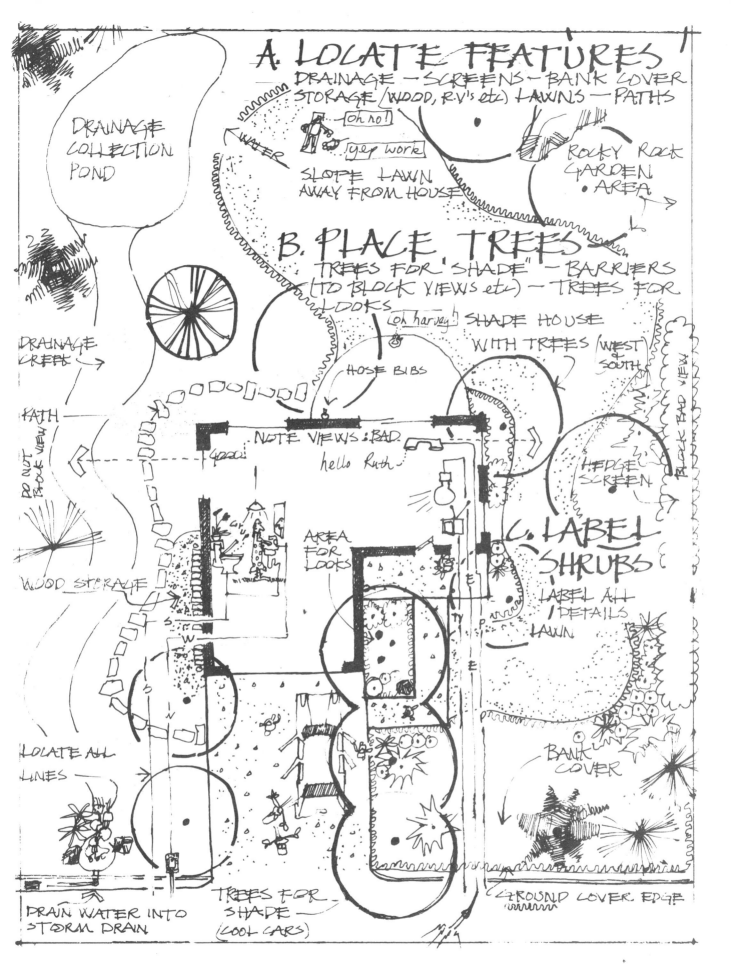

These are the steps in beginning a landscape plan.

it happens when people skip the land shaping process during landscaping, or they buy a house in the summer before the rains have exposed drainage problems. All of these problems can be solved by being aware of the importance of run off when landscaping or buying a house. If drainage concerns you, then read on in this section, and some simple solutions will be discussed such as the ol' 'Rube Goldberg' gravitational, perpetual motion pump that costs $5000 to install and takes ten inspectors to check! Most run off problems can be solved by sloping the ground away from the house to street gutters or ditches but not on to the neighbors yard. You can be liable for damages caused by heavy rains that wash dirt and bark into a neighbor's pool. This actually happened in my local area a few years ago. Slope lawns at a minium rate of a three inch drop for every ten feet of distance, and this will get the water off so you can still walk on it during a rain. One housing contractor ran all the downspouts from the gutters into the planters that proceeded to kill half the plants, so avoid this move. Anyway, check your property's elevations with a hand level and a long stick or pole to make sure the water will run across the lawn, into the collection pond, then down the landscaped creek to storm drain. A hand level is like a small rifle scope, but it has a bubble inside and a line used to site on the stick held by your helper. It is available for around $20 at survey supply shops. Mark these elevations on your plan and begin with some surface like a patio as 0' then mark, for example, a five foot high area as +5 or five feet above the patio, and low areas can be notated with minus numbers. Now on paper you can tell if the water will go where it is supposed to.

If parts of your property are flat, with nowhere to run the water, then water drainage solutions get more complicated, and the typical design methods are the following: (1) gradually sloping, landscaped drainage creeks; (2) burying special drainage pipe (4" plastic pipe with holes in it) that can collect surface and ground water; (3) building a landscaped collection pond where the land slopes to it and the water will soak into the ground if the soil is just right or run out into a landscaped creek; (4) or finally installing a sump pump that can sit at the bottom of the collection pond if the ground will not soak up the water fast enough or if there are no low areas to run the water to. Each solution depends on the land's particular formation and work this part out right with an expert if necessary.

Inherited Landscape

Sometimes landscapes are inherited when a home or business office is purchased. If the grounds look bad with crab grass growing up through the juniper that blocks the windows, or an irrigation system that rumbles then blasts water all over the house and on passing cars, then parts or the whole landscape may need to be redone. The procedures will be the same for making a master plan then design away by the process of elimination, addition, and simple correction. Decide which plants stay, where to add plants, and which ones can be moved. Look at other problems such as negative drainage; a lawn that was poorly installed with bumps, dips, and soil that would barely grow cactus; or night lights that come on when the doorbell is rung! If the problems are great, then it may warrant to redo the whole area

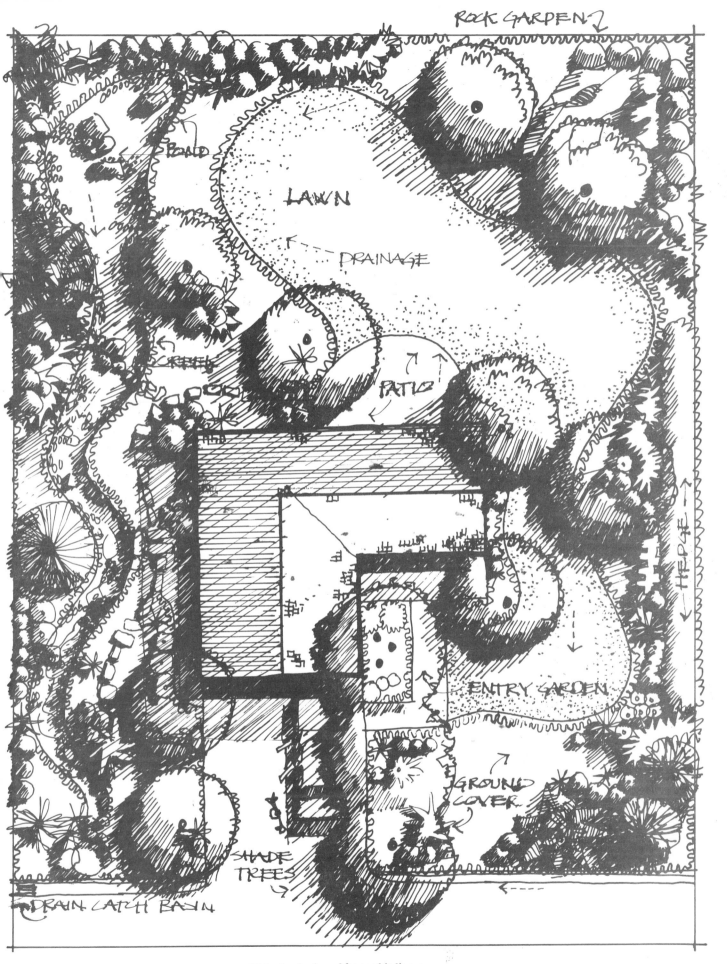

ROCK GARDEN

POND

LAWN

DRAINAGE

CREEK

PATIO

HEDGE

ENTRY GARDEN

GROUND COVER

SHADE TREES

DRAIN CATCH BASIN

This plan is viewed from a bird's eye.

with the exception of saving some trees and bushes.

If the landscape is basically sound then just replace some lawn areas with bushy shrub beds, add irrigation, plant some trees and bushes, and transplant good plants. Remove the bad plants such as the twenty foot juniper next to the front door that stinks, scratches, and just looks terrible. Entry ways should be surrounded by focal plants that are soft to the touch, neat in appearance, and seasonally blossom with fragrance. Make all of your plans on paper first since paper is cheap and follow the steps in chapter one.

Many times existing landscapes have too much lawn that runs right up to the house and fences, with scraggly grass that sticks up. Redesign an old square lawn in a neat curving fashion or angular pattern depending on your your taste for art and border it with neat shrub beds next to the house and property lines. Stake out the lawn surface to be converted into shrub beds and rent a sod cutter that is a weird machine that cuts grass into 18" strips. Another method is to spray the lawn to be removed with a hand pumper sprayer containing 'round-up' vegetation killer. Wait until the grass is 'completely' brown, add soil builders (fertilizer, lime, decomposed sawdust, etc.), rototill, and then rake before planting shrubs. This new grass shape and shrub bed can make a dull house perk up and come back to life!

Then revamp a sprinkler system that works fairly well by adding electric valves, timers, and new heads providing the pipe is good PVC or 'partially' rusted metal pipe, and there is plenty of water pressure. Take an old head to an irrigation supply store and see if an expert can match the head's

performance with a new one. Add new zones (valve and string of heads) if needed since the newly created shrub beds should ideally be watered separately from the grass areas. Redoing an existing landscape that is on good soil and was installed right, will cost considerably less than tearing it out and starting from scatch.

Well this concludes the design of your creation and now the rest is up to you. I know you can do it, so gather the design materials such as paper, tape measures, etc. and begin the design process. Some designers will use as many as ten overlays before choosing the right design, so use lots of tracing paper and in frustration, wad up bad designs and bounce them off the wall to help relieve mild psychological pressure derived from doing something new for the first time. This is a good blend of modern psychology and landscape design!. Some architects' offices fill up with wadded up tracing paper while intensely pursuing the ultimate design, so use up a few yards of rolled tracing paper.

Once your final design is chosen, then price it out as described next, and this step sends many designers right back to the drawing board. This is a common occurrence, so keep searching for the great design that fits the land like a glove, is within the budget, and will make you happy. If you are trying to create a flat lawn on a steeply sloping front yard, with a modest budget then you have set up an impossible design problem. Retaining walls, fill dirt, and lawns can get expensive, so lets be practical. Wad up that idea, bounce it off the wall, or pretend you are Larry Byrd and shoot them into the waste paper basket. Then get some more tracing paper, and try another idea. Paper is cheaper for trial and error than attempting to wad up a bad landscape project that is half built! Ok, lets get started now.

POND
ROCK GARDEN
CREEK
LAWN
PATIO
SHADE TREES
GROUND COVER
McNAIR 85'

This is a 3-d three dimensional version of the finished plan.

Cost

Now for the reality of landscaping. Use the materials, labor and equipment cost sheet to estimate the cost of your creation. The information below describes the methods used to figure square footage, cubic yards and how much fertilizer, grass seed, etc. to put on. If the total cost has devastated your budget, then redesign by: reducing shrub quantities and size; eliminating expensive details such as fountains, retaining walls, etc.; or plan to install the creation over a period of years. Do a quality job and don't skimp on soil preparation or irrigation. Remember, simple, basic designs cost less.

HOW TO FIGURE THE NUMBER OF SQUARE FEET.

Square or rectangle	multiply the length by the width (all measurements in feet)
Circle	3. 14 times the radius squared.
Triangle	$\frac{1}{2}$ times the base times the height.
Odd shapes	square them off and use the rectangle formula.

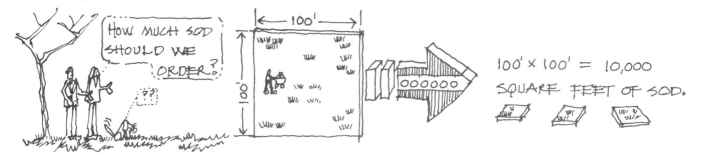

HOW TO FIGURE THE NUMBER OF CUBIC YARDS.

Multiply the length x the width x the depth (all in feet) then divide by 27 or simply multiply the area in square feet by the depth and divide by 27.

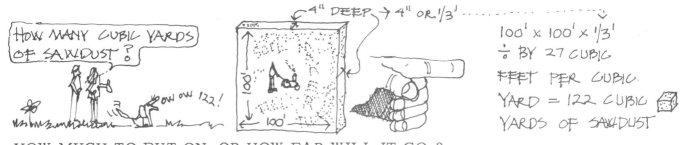

HOW MUCH TO PUT ON OR HOW FAR WILL IT GO ?

NOTE: FOR LIMESTONE, DOLOMITE, AND LIME SEE PAGE 29 AND 30

Grass seed	5 pounds	1000 square feet
Fertilizer (13-13-13)	10 pounds	1000 square feet
Caseron	5 pounds	1000 square feet
Round Up	1 quart	10,000 square feet
Soil Sulphur (acid)	20 pounds	1000 square feet lowers ph 1 point
Limestone (alkaline)	9o pounds	1000 square feet raises ph 1 point
Flat of ground cover	80 plants/12" on center	80 square feet
Bark or Rock cover	4" thick/10 cubic yards	810 square feet
Organic rototillers	10 pounds of heavy duty nightcrawlers	1000 square feet !! (joke)

MATERIALS ·· LABOR ·· EQUIPMENT

PROJECT *Medford Project* DATE PAGE *1*

Quanity	DESCRIPTON	Material $/unit	Total	Hourly $	Total	TOTAL $
15 yds.	Medium Bark Rock	$16.	delivery	25.		265.
15 yds.	Fine Bark	10.	"	" 25.	25.	175.
15 yds.	Aged Sawdust	10.	"	" 25	25	175
10 yds.	Granite, delivery included/10yds	5.5				55.
10 yds.	1/4" minus crushed rock "	7.00				70.
10 yds.	3/4" minus crushed rock "	7.00				70.
10 yds.	3/4"—1 1/2" drain rock "	7.00				70.
10 yds.	Pea Gravel "	7.00				70.
10 yds	Sand ↓ "	7.00				70.
10 yds	White crushed rock 1/2"	25.				285
10 yds	Top Soil - screened	7.5				75.
10 yds	Red or black cinder	18.				205
9.	Stepping stones 12"-cement ⬜⬜♡	2.60				23.4
10.	Stepping stones - flagstone	1.80				18.
10.	Lawn edging - cement 2'	1.00				10.
10.	Brick - red 7 1/2" long	39¢				3.9
100 ft.	Red wood 4" bender board	12¢				120.
100 ft	2x4 Pressure treated	32¢				32.
1 bun	12" wood stakes 50/bundle	2.85				2.85
10.	Black Pine Tree 6'	25.				250.
10.	Maple tree 6' to 8' B.&B.	16.				160.
10.	Shrub 1 gallon common	2.5				25.
10.	Shrub 5 gallon common	12.				120.
10.	Flat of ground cover	14				140.
10 lbs.	Grass seed	1.75				17.5
10.	Tree stakes 2"x2"x8'	1.00				10.
50 lbs	Caseron weed preventer	1.50				75.
1 Qt.	Round-up weed killer	34.				34.
80 lbs	Fertilizer	10¢				8.
80 lbs	Soil Sulphur	7.5¢				6.
80 lbs.	Lime	4¢				3.2
8 hrs.	Tractor-bucket-tiller-trailer			17.		156.
8 hrs.	Walk behind tiller - rear			9.5		76.
8 hrs.	Back hoe			16.25		130.
8 hrs.	Trencher - ride on			25.		200.
8 hrs.	Trencher - walk behind			12.		96.

Surfacing — **Steps** — **Edging** — **Plants** — **Chemicals** — **Equipment**

Here are some up to date prices, so your project can be estimated.

15

MATERIALS ·· LABOR ·· EQUIPMENT

PROJECT		DATE		PAGE		

Use this blank estimation sheet for your creation!

Quanity	DESCRIPTON	Material $ unit	Total	Hourly $	Total	TOTAL
		TOTAL				

chapter 2
PLANTING DESIGN

The ideal plant arrangement is where each plant is happy in its new environment and the whole planting bed radiates life with sparkling new growth, flowers, butterflies, birds and happy gardeners. It is a joy to have such a garden. This is what most gardeners strive to attain but few gain. With a little understanding and hard work, a vibrant planting arrangement is possible. Important factors that should be considered are: sun exposure; soil conditions; future plant size; flower color and season; plant leaf texture; plant color and plant purpose. If one factor is overlooked, the end result can be a mess. For example, if future size is overlooked, the garden may start out nice but problems may begin to occur as the years pass. One plant may stay tiny while the next plant grows huge and needs to be severely pruned, which can destroy the low maintenance, natural garden theory.

Plants should be carefully picked for the sun exposure, soil conditions and the wind element, or the plan is shot to begin with. Future size should be predicted so the spaces will eventually fill in with foliage and plants can express their natural form without pruning. Plant purpose should be planned, so barriers will be thorny, screens will be dense and courtyard plants will be showy. Leaf textures and colors should be arranged so uniformity and interest are created, otherwise it may be a drab mess or a cluttered extravaganza. Then if a person really wants perfection, flower colors can be blended and bloom times arranged so plants are blooming in a continuous sequence. The plant lists on the next few pages will help individuals pick the right plant for the situation.

Texture, color & shape are only some of the planting design factors.

17

Soil, Sun, Water Size

Most garden plants naturally grow some place on the earth where they have perfectly adapted to the conditions, such as: the Pacific rain forest; the windy, salt spray along the ocean; or the rough, dry desert. Now the key to planting design is to locate plants in an environment that reminds them of home or they might die from homesickness.

The plant list in this guide will help determine the natural condition that each plant prefers. The next step is to locate other plants that enjoy the same conditions so they can form a strong-growing, vibrant community. Most basic landscape gardens will have: dense shade, wet rain forest, plant communities; sunny, temperate plant beds; and the dry desert plant areas. Now the irrigation can be set heavy for all of the rain forest plants, such as ferns, azaleas, and rhododendrons, and light for the desert community. Each community will need the right amount of sun, special soil conditions and the correct amount of water. Generally, rain forest plant communities prefer rich deep, acid soil while desert plants, like Juniper, prefer sandy, rocky, alkaline soil. Windy areas should be carefully planned because the wind will burn some plants during the winter due to the 'chill factor.' For example, the temperature may be 30 degrees in the calm air, but the windy areas may read at 10 degrees on the thermometer, so keep this in mind.

Ground Covers

These plants provide the landscape with a lush, rich effect and help choke out invading weeds that enjoy ruining the best of landscapes. Ground covers prefer special conditions as described in the previous section on soil, sun, water and wind. Some ground covers are quick, vigorous spreaders, such as ivy, while others, like scotch moss, are slow, little delicate creepers. Use the vigorous ones to cover large areas and the slow creepers on little neat landscaped areas. The vigorous ones usually form a thick mat that will eventually choke out the weeds while the slow creepers may need frequent weeding while covering and even after established. Some ground covers spread by underground roots like Aaron's Beard St. John's Wart and lawns will be invaded if this plant is too close, so plant carefully. For a super landscape, establish ground covers on all of the shrub beds and eliminate the use of bark. Space the vigorous spreaders 1' on center; water them well; fertilize periodically; and weed often until the ground cover is thick and healthy. Most weeds will eventually die out unless a stubborn weed like crabgrass is present. These weeds must be completely eradicated with a spray before ground covers are planted. I believe in the long run, vigorous ground covers are less expensive than the 'bark route' when costs such as high bark prices, chemicals, weeding, bark replacement cost and general appeal are considered over a full-year period.

Study the plant list on the next few pages, consider the ideas described in this section, try some of your ideas and your landscape will improve with age.

The ultimate, go for it!

18

Shrubs Shrubs have many purposes other than growing out on to walks, covering windows, or scratching while you walk by. Well chosen shrubs can block the wind and bad views or keep kids from running across your yard. They can be thorny and prevent burglars from getting into the yard, or they can make your backyard a quiet, cozy escape from the hot, oily city scene by enclosing the lawn with a wall of green leaves and bright flowers. Once your private garden is complete then on the weekends or after work, you can play king of the jungle where all creatures are subject to your domination, including the dog who is vice king ninety percent of the time while you are working.

Shrubs will provide privacy along the property lines if they are tall and dense. The bushes next to the tall border should be shorter and colorful with various patches of flowers that will attract birds and butterflies. Then in front of the showy vegetation and next to the green lawn, a third row of short shrubs can be planted such as Spring Heath that will help fill in spaces created by the midrange shrubs. A wide vegetation border will cut down lawn area so mowing the lawn will be a fun job rather that a mowing marathon.

Bushes come in all sizes and shapes such as ones that grow tall like telephone poles, or ones that spread way out like mammoth starfish, so pick the ones that fit the space by using the plant charts. The ol' round peg in the square hole doesn't work in blocks or in landscaping, so use large bushes to fill big areas or tall narrow ones when a screen is needed in a five foot wide area. I perfer to use shrubs so their natural size and shape fits the space, so little pruning is needed. Some bushes grow huge with age like Fraser Photinias that are mistakenly used to fill five foot planter beds. These bushes will grow fifteen feet wide in good conditions, so don't under estimate the power of a bush. Please, what ever you do, don't plant Tam Junipers in a three foot wide planter, so in five years the natural mound form of this shrub will require severe pruning that permanently ruins the shape of the shrub, unless it is pruned in a bonzi tree manner. This planting error has been made at least one thousand times in Medford, Oregon, and probably in other cities too.

Sometimes small landscapes can be made to look larger by using an old Japanese gardener's trick. If you were in an airplane, people would appear to be very small along with trees that would have fine dots for leaves. Up close these objects are larger and some tree leaves are pancake size. This principle is applied in a garden by framing windows or garden view points with large leafed trees, such as a Norway Maples, or wide leafed shrubs, then leaf sizes should reduce as one looks to the end of the garden. The end of the garden should be composed of small leafed trees, like Japanese Maples, and fine leafed shrubs. This makes a small garden appear larger, so try this idea in your garden.

Create an illusion of space.

Tree Factors   In addition to the plant arrangement factors described earlier, trees have a few additional considerations. Roots, shade, wind breakage, leaf size, fall color and winter appearance should all be studied before a tree is picked. This means a lot of study and now you can appreciate professionals! Some trees have naturally shallow roots that will rob lawns and shrub beds of nutrients. Older homes have cast iron plumbing that can be clogged by tree roots and some trees, like poplars, are infamous for this. Other trees uproot patios and sidewalks. Some trees cast dark, dark shadows that starve lawns and some shrubs of light. Use tall deciduous trees to protect your home from the hot sun and to save the paint, then in the winter these trees allow passive solar heating. Use tall, stout evergreens, like Deodora Cedars, to protect your property from the cold winds. Certain trees should not be planted adjacent to buildings in windy areas because they grow fast and weak, then blow over onto homes and cars. Heavy limbs break off and crash below. Trees are beginning to sound like monsters! Just pick the right ones or they can be monsters. Now to end this tree marathon, pick trees that have beautiful fall color and nice winter structure in scenic areas and small leaves over ground cover.

Some trees can be enemies!

Plant Layout   Once the general landscape plan has been completed as described in chapter one, begin the detailed work of plant selection. One good way to begin is to make a list of plants that are doing well in your area since these plants already like the soil, sun, and other plant growing conditions. Some 'growies' just thrive in certain areas so pick the healthiest plants in your area, and you will have a good start on a plant list. Usually neighborhoods share similar soil conditions but check to make sure. Soils can be modified to suit most plants if the natural soils are poor, but it can be expensive. In the case of poor soils, decide whether your plants will be for the native poor soil or for improved soil. The two plant lists can be very different.(More on soils is in chapter four.) However, if the names of the plants aren't known, ask property owners, obtain some leaf samples, or take some pictures, and show them to the nursery owners for identification. Add to your list by shopping around nurseries and looking up plants in this guide.

Now, overlay your site plan with tracing paper as described in chapter one, and begin locating the trees first in some logical pattern with a purpose such as plugging the sewer, close to paving so they will up root the driveway, or next to the pool so you can add to the pool cleaning job! No, in all seriousness, this happens all the time by accident because some landscape designers are not familiar with the nature of the plants used. "Know thy plant" and have a tree work for you by shading the house and cars or by looking pretty away from the pool.

Draw in the trees on the plan first and then add the shrubs and ground covers in some well thought out logical pattern. This sounds

easy, but experts take years to become good at this part. Seasoned professionals even fuss over plant locations and quibble over which one will look best, because plants are like individual works of art, and everyone has a different opinion. Remember the basic purposes for shrubs are providing dense screens and barriers, covering the ground to prevent weed growth, and to look pretty. Draw the plants smaller than their full size on paper so they will grow together and use abbreviated labels as you go. For example, Phitzer Chinese Junipers can grow to twelve feet in diameter, but show them on the plan with nine foot diameter circles and label them "P.C. Jun. 9' o.c.". The "o.c." means on center or nine feet apart. Plants should grow together to form an interesting mass, and rather than using one here and one there, place plant types in various groups that blend in terms of color, size, shape, etc.. Plant three here, seven there, twenty five over there in the case of a screen, and one focal plant in a prime location to draw attention. Plants can be like a group of people, since there is always one who gets the attention by acting out or telling jokes! This method provides unity in the project by blending textures, colors... and provides attention getters that add interest. Try to visualize the colors, sizes, and textures of leaves as you go. Using one of everything or plugging in two hundred straight Tam junipers can really ruin a potentially neat home landscape, so use a little creativity.

Now decide which plants to make larger, otherwise a bunch of little gallon shrubs can look bleak out in the vast expanse of bark. If cost is not a concern, make most of the trees 15' plus and the shrubs five gallon size, then the landscape will mature quickly. Quality plants do cost a few dollars, for example a 12' by 60' planter will cost about $240, not including labor, if gallon shrubs are planted three feet on center and $900 if five gallon shrubs are planted three feet on center. Our leafy friends can add up in price!

One neat plant can be a focal point.

In conclusion, a landscape is like a big organic sculpture that takes years to finish, and to have a masterpiece one must know the conditions and the plants. Most experts have created landscape 'Frankensteins' by mistake, and this type of landscape just keeps growing worse, so prevent this by careful study. If the plants like their new home in the landscape, and the correct plants are mixed together then the plant sculpture will grow neater every year. The key is to know how the leafy sculpture will look as it grows towards maturity. Landscaping is like cooking rice and remembering the little critters will expand. I recall having tons of rice left over after cooking a good hearty dinner of 'rice pile off' or pilaf. Plants act the same way, since they expand, or they can die if they don't like their new homes. Simply put the right plant, in the right spot, to get the right effect.

STEP C: PLANT LIST

Scientific Name				
Common Name	Code Name	Condition		Quan.
		Size		
SHRUBS				
Juniperus chinensis pfitzeriana glauca BLUE PFITZER CHINESE JUNIPER	Blue Jun.	1 gal.		2
Juniperus chinensis 'Old Gold' OLD GOLD CHINESE JUNIPER	O.Gold Jun.	1 gal.		8
Juniperus chinensis pfitzeriana aurea GOLDEN PFITZER JUNIPER	G.P. Jun.	2 gal.		1
Mahonia aquifolium OREGON GRAPE	O.Grape.	1 gal.		5

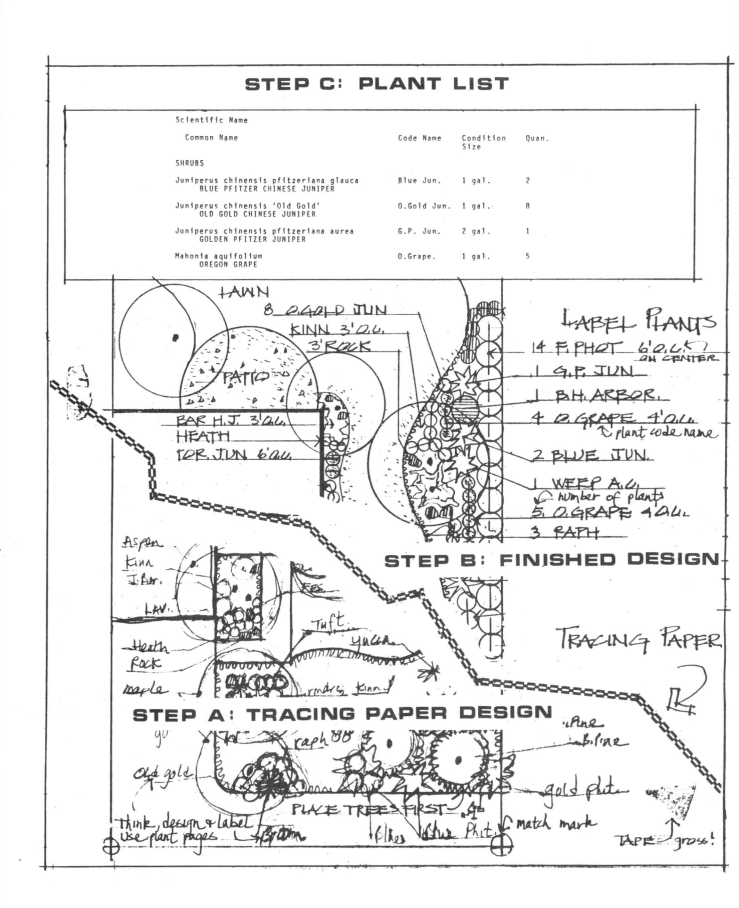

LAWN

8 O.GOLD JUN

KINN 3' O.C.

3' ROCK

PATIO

BAR H.J. 3' O.C.

HEATH

TOR. JUN 6' O.C.

LABEL PLANTS

14 F. PHOT 6' O.C. ON CENTER

1 G.P. JUN

1 B.H. ARBOR.

4 O.GRAPE 4' O.C. ← plant code name

2 BLUE JUN.

1 WEEP A.C. ← number of plants

5. O.GRAPE 4' O.C.

3 RAPH

STEP B: FINISHED DESIGN

Aspen

Kinn

J.Ber.

LAV.

Heath

Rock

maple

Tuft

Yucca

mdrs. Kinn

TRACING PAPER

STEP A: TRACING PAPER DESIGN

yu

raph

Old gold

think, design & label
use plant pages

Broom

PLACE TREES FIRST

F/kes

Blue Phot

match mark

Pine

b.fine

gold phot

TAPE ↑ gross!

These are the basic steps in planting plan layout.

22

Nature is a good example of plant design.

chapter 3
Now Build It

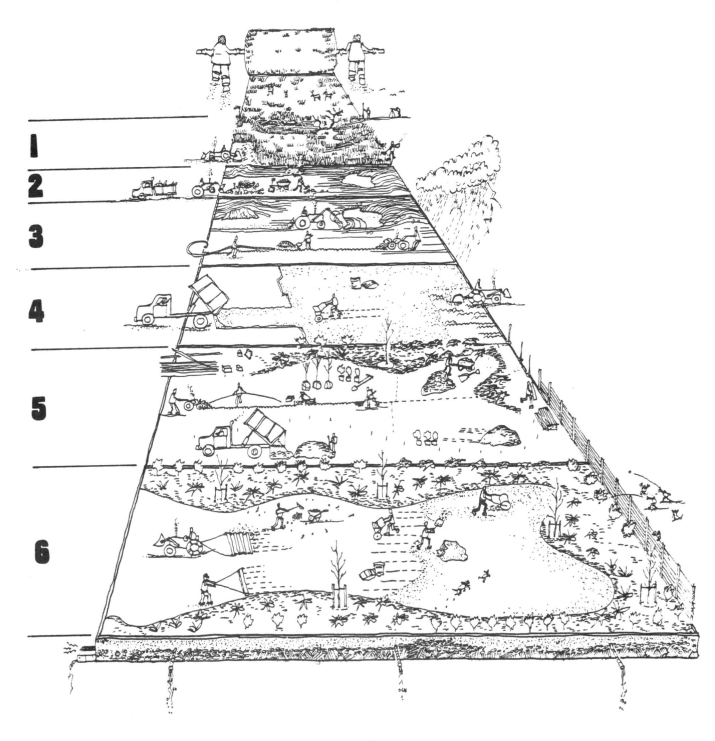

1

2

3

4

5

6

Work Sequence

Planning the work sequence helps prevent landscaping from turning into a nightmare, with piles of rock that need to be transported past finished fences, or lawns that have settled, leaving bumps and dips crisscrossed with trench lines. Planning and timing the landscape work with the weather can prevent vast amounts of unnecessary work.

Work Steps	Labor	Tools
1. Survey	A. Review the plans, obtain permits	Plans, 12" stakes
	B. Locate property lines and easements	12" stakes, 100' tape, hammer
2. Clearing	A. Spray and cut or cut weeds	Copy of property survey Tractor mower, round up spray weed eater, hand sickle, sprayer
	B. Pile debris and haul off or burn	Tractor and bucket, dump truck, wheelbarrow, shovel, rake, pitch fork
	C. Install electric power	Electric company
3. Grading	A. Grade land for drainage, shape	Tractor, bucket and rear leveler, top soil, shovel, wheelbarrow, pick, rake
	B. Install drain pipes and sump pumps	Trencher, sump pumps, drain pipe, wheelbarrow, wire, drain rock, trenching shovel
4. Soil preparation	A. Rototill soil and additives (aged sawdust, fertilizer, lime or soil sulphur)	Tractor and rear tiller, fertilizer spreader
5. Irrigation and Planting	A. Stake, install and test irrigation	100' tape, hammer, stakes, trencher, narrow trench shovel, steel rake, pick ax, wheel barrow, ax, hack saw
	B. Backfill trench, pack soil, soak, and fill settled areas	Square point shovel
	C. Plant trees, then shrubs	Plants, trees stakes, 10 gauge wire, hose pieces 6" long, wire cutters, can cutters, stake pounder bucket, vit. B, fertilizer, shovel, wheel barrow and aged sawdust
	D. Rake area, hoe weeds and apply caseron in shrub beds	Caseron, rubber gloves, bucket, steel rake, hoe
	E. Spread bark, cinder or other surfacing	Dump truck, wheelbarrow, wide shovel, rake
	F. Plant ground cover (no caseron)	Plants, trowel, knife, potting mix
	G. Finish paths, ponds, etc.	Rock, wheelbarrow, shovel, edging, sand, cement, pumps, drains, roller, wire mesh
6. Lawn	A. Finish grade lawn, remove rocks soak to settle, regrade	Tractor and level drag, hand pulled leveling board, steel rake, shovel, wheelbarrow
	B. Spread seed	Mechanical spreader
	C. Cover seed with mulch	Mulch, wheelbarrow, wide shovel
	D. Roll	Heavy roller
	E. Irrigate and keep damp	Irrigation system
	F. Check timer, weed and build fences	

Clearing Weeds

CLEARING

Before landscaping, all trash and debris should be hauled off or burned for obvious reasons. This can be quite a job, especially on new construction sites where sheet rock, boards, wire, and other items are scattered all over and imbedded in the mud. Some of these items can really fix a rototiller! The following will answer the weed removal questions:

TALL WEEDS:

Remove all rocks, branches, etc.; cut the gangling weeds with a tractor-powered rotary mower for large areas, or a weed eater for small areas. Hand sickles and rotary lawn mowers work in small areas providing the weeds are sparse, and you don't mind WORK! Rake up the weeds, haul off or burn right on the spot.

STUBBORN WEEDS:

PLants such as Poison Oak, Crab Grass, etc. should be destroyed, or they might grow back and ruin the best of landscapes. These scourges should be sprayed with a product called Round Up, over a period of years in the case of well established plants. Get a pump-up sprayer and spray on non-windy, hot days, and wait a week for the results. Respray plants that survived.

Grass Removal

There are two ways to remove existing lawn areas. If you want to use the lawn some where else, simply soak a dry lawn the day before, then rent a goofy machine called a sod cutter and strip off the grass in 12" to 18" wide strips. Roll up the sod, keep it damp, then roll it out where you want the grass after the soil has

been prepared as described in the grass section. If the grass is not needed, then spray the lawn with Round Up, wait at least a week until it has turned brown, soak the dead grass, then rototill it in and rake off the excess grass. The grass will provide organic matter to the soil and will decompose in time.

Grading Soil

The land should be sloped away from buildings, so the water will run off before it can puddle or flood buildings. This is the time to build mounds and other features like ponds and landscaped drainage creeks.

The best tool for sloping the land away from buildings, shaping mounds or making landscaped drainage creeks and ponds is a four wheel drive tractor with a front bucket and a grading blade on the back that levels out the dirt. Before getting carried away, pull out your plans made from chapter one and stake in the important features by measuring straight out from the building and scaling from the plan. Now rent the tractor and rough grade the slopes then store any scraped off topsoil in one area, so it can be used for lawns and shrub beds later. Slope the land away from the house and walks in such a manner that the water will run off the property and out to the street, but not onto the neighbor's property. Use the tractor to cut the dirt down in some areas and add dirt with the thought of keeping the water moving. The ground should be sloped with a three inch drop to every ten feet that makes the slope some what invisible. Steep slopes are not attractive looking, and slopes less than minimum cause soggy lawns and shrub beds. Measure the slopes with a hand level while tractor grading. Now if the land form will not permit the water to run off, then drainage pipe may be required, and this will be discussed in the next few pages.

After rough grading, restake features, then form ponds and creeks and use the excess dirt to fill in low areas or to build mounds along the creek. If you have a large area, then rent a good sized tractor and do all the land sculpturing or grading in one furious day. Just don't get carried away and rip the siding off your house, dig up your power line and execute yourself for the crime of being inexperienced, or back into local kids watching all the excitement. Renting a tractor is fun because you have immense power over moving dirt that would have taken days with the misery stick (shovel) and wheelbarrow. If you plan this part right, the tractor could be used to haul materials such as big piles of rock or bark and to rototill in the soil additives after the grading is done. Have the rental company attach the tiller on the back rather than the grading blade and use the front bucket for digging and leveling the dirt. Level by backing up the tractor and dragging the bucket.

Use equipment to move heavy materials.

Thinking here can save lots of work, so use the front bucket to move materials such as sawdust, bark, and creek rock from the front to the back yard where it can be handled from there with the ol' wheelbarrow and shovel routine. All of this needs to be coordinated with the weather, tractor rental, and the material deliveries. Moving ten yards of drain rock with a wheelbarrow because the tractor was due back to the rental company, can create a strong back and a weak mind!

The best tool for installing drainage pipe other than your basic shovel is the gas powered trencher that is like a big dirt chain saw. Rent a trencher, slope the trench out to the street, and check the grade with the hand level unless you have a method to run water up hill! Dig it a little deeper than necessary to allow for three inches of rock on the bottom. If the ditch's depth will be much over two feet, then a four wheel drive trencher or small backhoe with a narrow bucket is needed.

Teeth on the trenchers can be set with great difficulty, to cut various widths of trench, and 4" pipe must easily fit into the trench, so measure the width between the trencher teeth before renting one, to avoid problems I had once. The pipe had to be forced into the ditch since my trencher cut a little under, a four inch ditch. These little oversights can cause a normal human being to turn into a red faced baboon that runs around the back yard howling and screaming!

Now that the trench is dug, finish grade with a misery stick (shovel) while checking the grades with a hand level, and place a 3" bed of drainrock in the bottom to bring it up to grade. The four inch black corregated pipe should be set on a minium grade of a 3" drop to 10' run and the smooth walled, rigid drainfield pipe can be set flatter with a 1" drop per 10'. Why? Corregated pipe collects dirt and plugs up if water barely trickles through it. Set the pipe in with the holes 'down', make the connections when needed, keep it on grade without bending up in spots like a camel, especially with the flexible pipe, and backfill with the drain rock.

If you want the pipe to catch surface water, then bring the rock up to the surface and install wood dirt catchers as shown in the nearby drawing, otherwise cover the rock with topsoil. Now that took a while to explain and some readers are probably bored to tears. Just think how you will feel after you spend $4000 on landscaping, just to see it mush down in standing water and turn into a winter disaster because this section was skipped over. So lets stretch, wake up, then reread any section you glossed over. The next section covers making the soil just right for your plants.

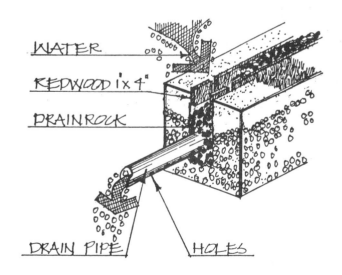

Use drainpipes when the land is relatively flat.

SOIL CONDITIONING

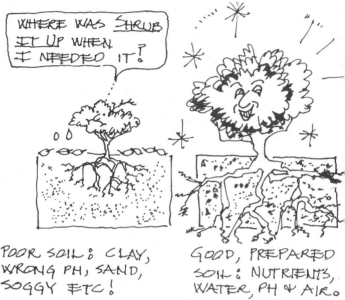

POOR SOIL: CLAY, WRONG PH, SAND, SOGGY ETC!

GOOD, PREPARED SOIL: NUTRIENTS, WATER, PH & AIR.

Prepare the soil right, then plant.

If plants don't like their new homes, they let you know by barely growing and looking awful or by shriveling up and dying, so lets not allow this to happen. The main idea of soil preparation is to provide plants with the proper soil that is loose enough for roots to grow, will hold water and nutrients, will allow excess water to pass through, has rich nutrient content, and has the right chemical balance in terms of PH or acid-alkaline ratio. That is really a mouth full! If any of these factors are overlooked then plant performance may be severely retarded, unless special plants are used that prefer less than ideal conditions. For example, Red Alder trees prefer soggy and wet soil since they naturally grow next to and in creeks. However, most nursery plants reqiure soil that has been prepared right or you can't expect super results.

Generally plants will really take off if they are grown in the right soil, and if they receive the proper amount of sun and water. Good friable top soil that crumbles when a damp ball is thrown against a wall (good soil test) usually has most of the features mentioned above. If the soil ball sticks on the wall, it has too much clay, or if it breaks before it hits the wall, then the soil is too sandy. This is one of the more scientific tests!

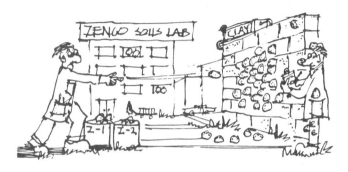

The ultimate scientific soil test!

POUNDS OF LIMESTONE PER 1000 SQUARE FEET NEEDED TO BRING THE PH TO 6.5 (optimum PH)			
PH	SANDY LOAM	LOAM	CLAY
4.0	115 LBS.	160 LBS.	230 LBS.
4.5	95 "	135 "	195 "
5.0	80 "	105 "	150 "
5.5	60 "	80 "	105 "
6.0	30 "	40 "	55 "

Amount of limestone to add.

Test the soil for nutrients and PH with a $15 kit that can be purchased at a garden supply store. Nutrients (nitrogen, phosphorus, potassium and other elements) provide grow power for the plant and the proper PH (lime or sulfur) enables the plant to absorb the nutrients which is rather important! Nutrients have to go into the plant to do any good. Most soils will benefit by spreading 20 pounds of 8-8-8 fertilizer per 1000 square feet. (The first 8 means 8% of the whole bag is nitrogen, then the next percentage is phosphorus, then finally potassium.)

Desert soil is usually akalkine or has a high lime content, and rain forest soil is usually acid because the lime has been washed out. A PH test uses a number rating with 7 as neutral, above 7 is alkaline, and below 7 is acid. Most garden plants grow well in slightly acid soil or a PH of 6.5. Rain forest plants, like ferns, Rhododendrons, and Azaleas really like acid soils while desert plants, like Junipers, prefer alkaline soils. Add limestone to soil that is too acid and add soil sulfur to soil that is too alkaline. Straight lime is different from limestone since lime is more potent and less of it is needed to do the job. The next page has how much limestone or sulfur to add for raising or lowering the PH. Hope this is simple to understand because it is important.

We have discussed the foundation for a landscape, grading and soil preparation, now we will move on. If the foundation is weak then guess what? The Italian builders of the 'Leaning Tower of Piazza' found out when their building almost fell over and the same thing may happen to a potentially good landscape, so establish a good foundation to build from.

Prepare a good soil foundation before building!

STICKY CLAY: Sticky gumbo that builds up on your shoes has locked in growing power that needs to be released before most plants will grow in it. Clay is composed of ultrafine particles that must be mixed with larger particles such as sawdust or sand. Cover the soil with

SOIL ADDITIVES

TABLE ANALYSIS AND USE OF SOME COMMON FERTILIZER MATERIALS

Name of Material	Analysis N-P-K	Other Nutrients	Rate of Application Dry	Effect on pH
PRIMARY FERTILIZERS				
Ammonium sulfate	20-0-0	S	1/2-1 lb./100 sq. ft.	Very Acid
Ammonium nitrate	33-0-0		1/4-1/2 lb./100 sq. ft.	Acid
Urea CO $(NH_2)2$	46-0-0		1/4-1/2 lb./100 sq. ft.	Sl. Acid
Superphosphate	0-20-0	Ca+S	3-8 lbs./1,000 sq. ft.	Neutral
ADDITIVES				
Limestone, Dolomitic (1)	none	Ca+Mg	5-20 lbs./100 sq. ft.	Basic
Hydrated Lime Ca(OH)$_2$	none	Ca	2 lbs./100 sq. ft.	Basic
Gypsum (calcium sulfate) CaSO$_4$	none	Ca+S	2-5 lbs./100 sq. ft.	Neutral
Sulfur	none	S	1-2 lbs./100 sq. ft.	Acid
Epsom salts (magnesium sulfate)	none	Mg+S	8-12 oz./100 sq. ft.	Neutral
Aluminum sulfate	none	S	1 tsp./6" pot	Very Acid
COMPLETE				
Complete dry (mixtures)	13-13-13	Var.	2 lbs./100 sq. ft.	Various
Organic	5-10-3	Var.	2-4 lbs./100 sq. ft.	Various
ORGANICS				
Poultry manure	3-2-2	Many	20 lbs./100 sq. ft.	
Steer manure	1-0.5-2	Many	50 lbs./100 sq. ft.	
Activated sewage sludge (2)	5-4-0		3-5 lbs./100 sq. ft.	Acid
Animal tankage	7-9-0		3-4 lbs./100 sq. ft.	Acid
Castor pomace (poisonous)	5-1-1		3-5 lbs./100 sq. ft.	
Cottonseed meal	7-2-2		3-4 lbs./100 sq. ft.	Acid
Dried blood	12-0-0		2-3 lbs./100 sq. ft.	Acid
Hardwood ashes	0-1-5		1-1.5 lbs./100 sq. ft.	Basic
Hoof and horn meal	13-0-0		2-3 bls./100 sq. ft.	
Linseed meal	5-1-1		3-5 lbs./100 sq. ft.	Acid
Seaweed (kelp)	2-1-15		2-3 lbs./100 sq. ft.	
Soy Bean meal	6-1-1		3-5 lbs./100 sq. ft.	
Steamed bone meal	3-20-0		5 lbs./100 sq. ft.	Basic
Fish emulsion	6-2-1			
Fish Meal	5-1-1 to 10-5-5			
Rabbit	1-0.3-0.6		20-40 lbs./100 sq. ft.	

(1) Not less than 40% Magnesium Carbonate
(2) Milorganite® a treated sewage sludge, unsuitable for edibles due to heavy metals.

NOTE→ Lime is also called slaked or hydrated lime and don't use a type of lime called quick, burnt, or caustic lime. ✳!!✳

WOOD ASHES

10-15 lbs./1,000 sq. ft. annually, depending on kind of wood burned. Monitor potassium levels in garden and do not use ashes where K is adequate as they contain high percentages. Ashes raise pH only slightly: it requires 68 lbs./1,000 sq. ft. to raise 1 point.

3 gal. pail = approximately 10 lbs.
1 cup = approximately 4 oz.

Using Wood Ashes in the Home Garden, Extension Bulletin FG 61.

ADJUSTING pH for each 100 sq. ft. of clay:

3½ lbs. lime or 5½ lbs. dolomite or 6 lbs. limestone raises by 1 unit.

2 lbs. sulfur or 6½ lbs. aluminum sulfate or 7½ lbs. iron sulfate lowers by 1 unit.

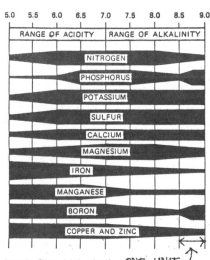

FIGURE 3.—Effect of change in pH on the availability of plant nutrients.

✳ ✳
NOTE: LIMESTONE IS CALCIUM CARBONATE; DOLOMITE IS CALCIUM MAGNESIUM CARBONATE OR MAGNESIUM RICH LIMESTONE OR POWDERED WHITE MARBLE; LIME IS CALCIUM HYDROXIDE THAT IS THE END PRODUCT OF QUICKLIME AND WATER. SEA SHELLS CRUMBLE AND FORM LIMESTONE.

6" of aged sawdust or sand and add some fertilizer and till until the soil becomes fluffy. Keep adding sand until the soil becomes friable, otherwise it may become cement-like. If the clay is bone dry, soak the area after the additives have been spread, then till or the tiller will bounce and jerk for hours without tilling. If fresh sawdust is used, then add extra fertilizer and continue to do so for years because it robs the soil of nitrogen when it decomposes.

CRUDDY, ROCKY SOIL: If your soil has been cursed with this, indicated by the neighbors growing only prickly junipers and large boulders, then don't despair. Dig a hole and check for a hardpan under the surface. The hardpan must be ripped up by using a 'cat' with deep rippers. Level drag the surface with a tractor, rake the surface rocks up, load into the tractor's bucket and haul off. Cover the site with 3" of topsoil and lightly till in without kicking up lots of rocks; then add three more inches of topsoil for lawns and 9" for shrub beds. The two soils must be lightly tilled as mentioned, otherwise water and roots tend to stop when a distinct division occurs between two soils. Save the rocks for accent features later in the landscape.

SANDY SOIL: This soil is too porous and the water and nutrients run right through the soil before plants can benefit. It also dries out quickly after watering. Spongy material like decomposed sawdust needs to be added. Till in 6" of decomposed sawdust and the soil should be ideal for plants.

TOPSOIL: If the soil has been compacted, then rototill it until it becomes fluffy.

Sprinklers

Now, pull out the irrigation plans and double-check the layout with what is on the ground. Half of the battle is a well designed plan that avoids tree roots, rock and minimizes trenching by utilizing heads that throw a large radius of water. This is the time to make last-minute changes. The following will provide the 'do-it-yourselfer' with a good, basic set of irrigation installation guidelines. If problems arise, hire a consultant.

1. STAKING: With a 100' tape, 12" stakes and a hammer, mark where each irrigation head will be located. Then, with a colored stake, mark the trench lines so when everything is staked it isn't a confusing mess of stakes.

2. UTILITY LINES: Mark where all utility lines cross the trench lines, so the trencher can be raised at these points, otherwise it is a shocking discovery when the trencher finds a shallow electric line.

Discovering wires can be a Shocker!

3. TRENCHING: Now comes the fun part and for your sake, I hope the soil is soft and free of rocks and roots or you are in for lots of groveling in the dirt. At this point you can hire a contractor, rent a trencher or hire some kids with shovels, depending on the conditions. The following is when to do which: With gently rolling lawn, rent a walk-behind trencher or hire the kids. Rent a medium-sized trencher and soak the trench lines with a soaker hose if the soil is dry; with acres and acres of rolling hills, rent a trencher with four-wheel drive; with steep ground, rent a walk-behind trencher that can be easily maneuvered and trench down hill; with bottomless mud, hire the kids or wait until the soil dries out or the

Hillside trenching can have its "ups and downs!"

trencher will get bogged down; with bedrock or large boulders, hire a trenching contractor because this job will require lots of know-how.

The trenches should be 12" deep in areas that occasionally freeze and deeper in colder areas. Lay the pipe soon after trenching or parts of the trench may cave in, especially after rainstorms, as I found out the hard way. For burrowing under walks, attach a 4' long piece of pipe to a garden hose and use it as a hydraulic drill. Pull up the trencher right away when large rocks are hit or it might break, which does not go over real big at rental businesses. To be safe, wear rubber boots just in case an electric line is cut.

For burrowing unders walks, use a pipe with a nozzel for a water drill.

4. IRRIGATION PARTS: Now pick up the irrigation parts from the nursery that designed your system or go shopping at some plumbing supply store that specializes in irrigation parts.

5. PIPE FITTING: Now put together the system like a kid gluing together a model airplane kit. Remember to use primer and the right glue on all joints because ABS glue comes in the same type of can as PVC glue, but using the wrong glue will ruin your sense of humor when it comes undone underground. Install pop-up heads flush with the ground by using 'cut off riser' or 'funny pipe.' Push the wire and pipe to the bottom of the trench and bury them in spots about 10' apart, but leave the head areas uncovered. Cave-ins will fall on top of the pipe and more pipe can easily be added if dry spots show up after testing. It would be wise to hire a plumber to connect the system to the main line because the pipe is usually rusted and 3' deep. You will not be real popular around the house if the connection is not made by dark, one more part is needed, the stores are closed and the water is off! Play it safe.

6. FLUSHING: Make sure the heads are not connected and turn on one valve at a time for five minutes until all the dirt is washed out. Use the timer for this and test it, too. If the last head pipes are dry, then plug the first few until the pressure builds and pushes all the dirt out the end. Lots of time will be wasted cleaning heads if dirt is left in the lines.

Even if you do get wet, blow all of the dirt and rocks out of the lines!

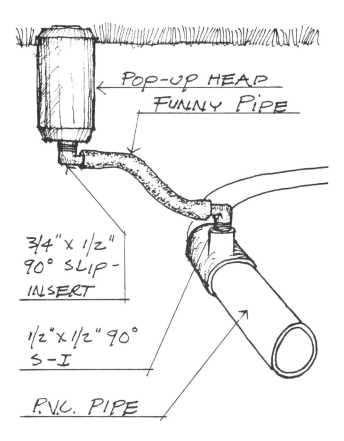

POP-UP HEAD
FUNNY PIPE

3/4" x 1/2" 90° SLIP-INSERT

1/2" x 1/2" 90° S-I

P.V.C. PIPE

"Funny pipe" head connection.

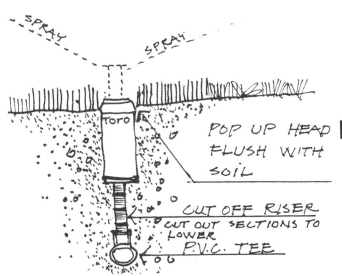

SPRAY
SPRAY

Toro

POP UP HEAD FLUSH WITH SOIL

CUT OFF RISER
CUT OUT SECTIONS TO LOWER
P.V.C. TEE

"Cut off riser" head connection.

7. TESTING: Put on the heads and bury them at the correct level and point them in the right direction. Turn on the valves one at a time and check for coverage, then add lines and heads later if dry areas occur. If the timer turns on each head, then things are looking up, but if one valve fails to respond, it might be dirt in the valve; a cut wire; a faulty timer. Hire an expert if the problem doesn't surface.

8. BACKFILLING: Rake or shovel the dirt in on the pipe and keep the rocks off the pipe. Pack the dirt by walking on it and run the wheel barrow tire along the trench. Turn on the sprinklers and soak the dirt until it settles the fill in the low spots. Make sure the line has completely settled because it looks tacky later when the trench lines show all over the lawn. Remove excess dirt, seed, mulch, roll and water the lawn until the bare trench lines fade into the sparkling green lawn.

Planting Trees & Shrubs

First plant the big heavy trees before planting the little shrubs all over; otherwise the shrubs get trampled in the process. Cut metal containers with tin snips, bury peat containers with the bottom cut out and bury ball and burlaped trees; then cut the top wrapping strings. If the soil is poor, add one part decomposed sawdust to one part native soil and mix completely for the planting mix. The plant depth is critical, so make sure the container surface is one inch under the bark topping when finished. Now water in the plant until the entire root area is saturated. Mix Alaska fish fertilizer and vitamin B root stimulator in a bucket and give each plant a gallon of grow power. Transplanting shock will kill some plants and the watering and fertilizer mix pulls the plants out of shock. In soggy areas, plant the trees and shrubs higher, then mound up the dirt so they will not drown later. Begin the shrub planting in the back and work to the front of the planter.

Store plants in the shade before planting and keep them wet. Ball and burlaped plants should be stored in damp sawdust. Flats of ground cover should be planted after the bark has been spread, otherwise the bark covers the little plants. Trees should be staked as shown in the tree planting diagram. Use a pipe pounder on the stakes. (4" x 2' pipe and cap)

The best time to plant is during the plant's dormant phase, which is from October to April. Nice ball and burlaped plants are available in the nurseries and transplanting success is very good. The rain naturally waters the plants and the cool temperature reduces the water demand. The roots grow in the relatively warm soil while the upper part of the plant remains inactive. During this time, inexpensive bare-root trees are available. A 6' to 8' bare-root tree will cost around $10. Then later after April, the same tree is transferred to a container and sold for around $15. Bare-root trees must be planted correctly or their chances for survival are greatly reduced. Later as the summer arrives, transplanting becomes more tricky because the plants are subjected to the bright sun and dry weather. The plants are adapted to the nice shady, cool nursery. Many times plants are overwatered during the hot weather which rots the fine root hairs and reduces the plants' ability to take in water. The plant then wilts and more water is dumped on it and finishes the rotting process. Plants should be initially watered in with lots of water to soak the root area and to cave in air pockets that can dry out roots underground. Then later the soil should be checked by digging down rather than looking at the dry surface soil for moisture clues.

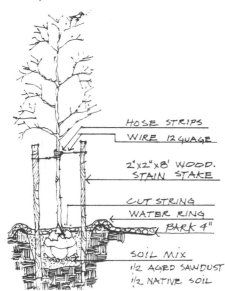

Ball and burlap tree planting.

Container planting method.

Step 1: Bareroot tree planting.

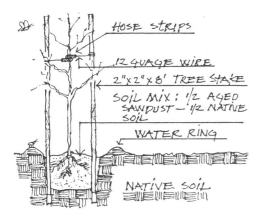

HOSE STRIPS

12 GUAGE WIRE

2"x2"x8' TREE STAKE

SOIL MIX: 1/2 AGED SAWDUST - 1/2 NATIVE SOIL

WATER RING

NATIVE SOIL

Step 2: Bareroot tree planting.

FERTILIZING

Too much fertilizer will burn off the root hairs also, so be careful and use a slow-release fertilizer or an organic fertilizer such as fish fertilizer. Slow-release fertilizer is hot fertilizer with a plastic coat that dissolves at various rates. Hot fertilizer dissolves all at once and burns the roots. I recently burned an old Daphne and the Vinca under it by overdoing the fertilizer and now some of the leaves have turned brown and fallen off. Another lesson in the school of 'hard knocks'! The guy on the next block fertilized his lawn with ground sterilent which kills everything, and was real puzzled when the lawn died in the front and back. He later realized the wrong chemical had been used while filling the fertilizer bucket in the dark. One should be careful with chemicals!

Weed Control, Bark & Edging

Smooth the planting bed surface after planting the trees and shrubs and hoe out any sprouting weeds. Apply the weed preventing caseron so each grain is about ½" apart and keep it real sparse around the tree and shrub root area. Spread it by hand and use rubber gloves, since the caseron is rather toxic smelling. Caseron will seep downhill and damage lawns, seed beds and ground cover areas, so put it on real thin above these areas. Do not apply caseron to seed beds or ground cover areas since it kills sprouting seeds for months and seems to retard sensitive plants like fragile ground covers and certain shrubs like junipers. Cover the caseron with 4" bark, which keeps it cool in the summer, since it turns into a gas rapidly with heat which can harm plants.

The bark cover provides a nice finished look, retards weeds that survive the caseron and helps retain moisture in the soil, so a good thick covering is recommended. Bark has gone up in price, so use 3" of fine bark as the first layer then top it with 1" of the more expensive 'bark rock' that comes in fine, medium or coarse. If price is not a factor, then use 4" of the 'bark rock' and eliminate the fine bark. The 'bark rock' lasts longer since all wood material eventually decomposes back to soil where weeds can root in. The coarser bark prevents the weeds from getting a foothold, and decomposes at a slower rate, while the fine bark returns to soil in a few years. The 'bark rock' will not scatter with the wind like fine bark does when it dries out, so keep this in mind if wind is a factor. Cinder, pebbles and crushed rock are substitutes for bark and are less expensive in certain areas, so use them freely, but fit the colors and textures into the overall design.

EDGING

Brick, cement, metal or three layers of redwood ¼" bender board can be used to edge the surface mulch and to define the lawn edge. The edging should be level with the lawn surface, so the mower can cut over it. Novice landscapers set one thin layer of redwood edging 3" above the lawn that makes mowing a real chore, and the wood soon cracks after the kids step on it. Look at the diagrams and install the edging right. Bark should be 1" below sidewalk surfaces otherwise it scatters out onto the walks and looks terrible, so excavate before placing the bark or rock. Edging is not required for informal landscapes.

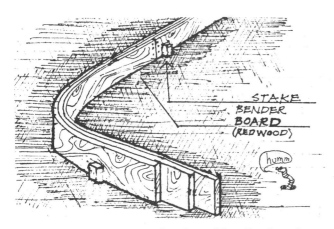

Try three layers of redwood bender board for lawn edging.

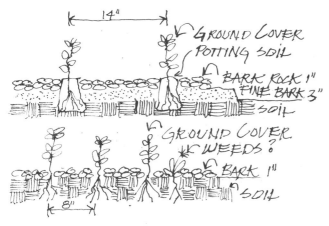

Here are some ground cover planting methods.

Planting Ground Cover

The trees, shrubs and bark or rock surfacing are in place now, and it is time to plant the ground cover. Cut the flats of ground cover into individual plants by using a knife and place some potting soil into a wheel barrow. With a trowel, push the bark back; dig a long narrow shaft by pushing the trowel back and forth. Hold a plant at the right level, backfill around the plant with potting mix, pack in, then return the bark or rock in place. One down and 500 to go, Oh no! Hire someone to help and the time will go by faster. If the ground cover is going to be planted close together so it will cover fast, then the bark or rock surfacing may not be needed and the potting mix can be eliminated if the soil is good. This will save time for large areas, but on steep banks the surface may wash off during rainstorms and ruin the ground

cover unless a good thick layer of coarse bark exists to hold the soil. Consider these factors when deciding. Fine ground covers like Scotch Moss should be cut into 1" by 1" squares, since the flat is one big massive plant. Keep the ground cover beds wet, fertilize and weed until the plants cover.

Lawns: Seed or Sod

SEED LAWNS

The best time to plant lawns is during a warm spring, but quality lawns can be achieved during the heat of summer if one is careful. Assuming the soil has been prepared as described in the soil preparation section, then seeding the lawn should be a simple operation. The following steps will lead to a quality lawn:

1. FINISH GRADING: For large areas, use a tractor and a rear leveling drag to flatten the surface. Pass back and forth until the surface is flat, then rake and remove all the surface rocks. For small areas, a hand pulled leveler works fine and is nothing more than an 8' long, two by twelve with ropes tied to each end and weights placed on top. Soak the entire area until the soft ground settles, then relevel. This is the foundation for a quality lawn, so do a good job here.

2. EDGING: Install edging as described in previous sections.

3. SEED: Pick the correct seed for your conditions, determined mainly by the amount of sun or shade the lawn will receive, and begin the seeding process. Use a mechanical spreader and put on a little more than recommended, so the lawn will fill in good and thick. Make sure sunny days are forecasted, otherwise a rainstorm may wash off the seed.

4. MULCHING: Cover the entire lawn with 1/8", and no more, of aged sawdust or peat moss. This can be done by shoveling the mulch from a wheelbarrow and throwing the mulch into the air and allowing it to settle in fine layers. If a breeze is blowing, throw it downwind or guess what? That's right, the mulch blows in your face!

5. ROLLING: Rent a lawn roller and roll the entire surface, so the seed will be in good contact with the soil, otherwise it sprouts and tends to dry up.

6. WATERING: This is the tricky part, for the lawn must remain damp throughout the day and should dry out before dusk, so it won't mildew at night. If too much water is put on, then the mulch and seed may wash off. The day the seed 'pops' or germinates is when the watering must be closely regulated or the seed can die within a few hours during hot weather. Look closely at the seed each day to see if it is germinating. Some seeds, like Annual Rye, germinate within a week, while others go for two weeks, depending on the amount of sun. Set computer timers to come on for three or four short intervals during the day and manually operate other systems to do the same. Some patient experts achieve good results by watering with a garden hose! One man had a nice thick lawn within weeks because he was right there watering "the day it popped," as he explained to me.

7. FOLLOW-UP: Once the lawn is established, cut the water back to once a day, mow, weed and fertilize.

The lawn should turn out lush and green providing the soil was prepared right, fertilizer and pH adjusters were added as needed, and the described steps were followed.

SOD LAWNS

Sod lawns make a nice instant effect and eliminate some of the risk factors encountered with seed lawns. Sod lawns can be laid in the hot summer or during the rainy winter with good results. Follow the steps up to number two for seed lawns, which includes finish grading and edging. The following describes the steps for sod lawns:

1. Soil preparation and pH adjusting are the same as for a seed lawn.
2. Grading, edging and rolling are the same as for a seed lawn.
3. Sod can be ordered directly from growers, providing the minimum of 1000 square feet is ordered. The sod is delivered at a specified time and payment is due on delivery. Buy small quantities of sod from some nurseries.
4. Start at the back edge of the lawn and work to the front edge. Simply unroll the sod and keep the joints tight and staggered. Overlapped edges can be trimmed with a scallop-edged kitchen knife. Save the excess pieces for filling in spaces as you go.
5. Keep the sod damp for at least three weeks until it has rooted into the soil. Hot weather can dry out sod that has not rooted in, so regulate the watering.

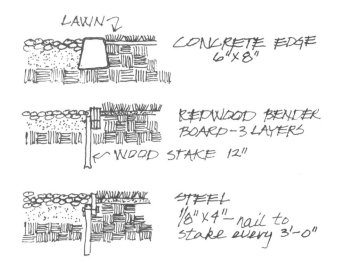

Set the bender board to the right height so you can mow over it.

This may happen if you hire a nurd!

chapter 4
SPRINKLER DESIGN HINTS

Irrigation design can be tricky in some cases, and it would take fifty pages to explain every situation, however we will cover planning the simple home system. The materials for the typical home system will cost anywhere from $300 to $700, and that includes a computer timer, pop-up heads, backflow preventers, etc. Backflow preventers? Yes, these protect public water systems, and we will cover what they are for later on.

If you cannot afford irrigation, then put it in later, after you get tired from frantically dragging hoses around in an attempt to prevent the 104 degree weather from turning your jungle back to desert! For a temporary system, string up soaker hoses for the shrub beds, and use the plastic movable Rain Bird impact heads in a series for the lawn. Hook up all the required hoses with the "Y" connectors at the hose bib.

For a reasonably priced system, consider hiring a nursery landscape contractor for providing a detailed, quality design. Provide prints of your plans that can be made at most drafting supply stores. Make arrangements with the nursery to order and deliver the irrigation parts, then install your own system. Hire the nursery expert to inspect your progress every so often, and you will save some money yet still have a quality system.

However, if you are a stubborn "do it yourselfer" who wants to design and install, and you have the technical perseverance to stick with the following irrigation design section then read on. Sprinkler design should not be too technical for most readers, but it may take a few readings and some patience until the principles sink in. Don't give up the first time through. Like most fields of endeavor, basic principles are involved that must be comprehended prior to proceeding or disaster usually follows!

The most basic principle of irrigation deals with water beginning in a pipe under pressure, and after each foot it moves, some pressure is depleted which is known as "friction loss." The water particles or molecules are roundish critters, and they rub against the walls of the pipe which slows them down, just as you would be slowed down while running down a hall with other people while rubbing against the wall. Next, the larger the pipe while the pressure remains the same, then less pressure is depleated for each foot of travel because fewer particles are rubbing against the wall. See, simple so read on.

Now, if the pipe is capped at the other end, then of course the pressurized water will not move and will split the pipe if the pressure is great enough. Next, we drill a hole and add an outlet such as a sprinkler, then we have water movement. As pressure is increased, squirting distance increases, until misting occurs and distance drops which is not good out in the yard. A pressure reducer needs to be added. As each outlet is added then the faster the movement until the water is traveling too fast. With excessive pressure and too many outlets, the pipe will vibrate radically since the water velocity is high, and if the water is suddenly shut off, the water will echo from end to end violently which is known as "water hammer." This phenomenon is not too cool and will spit pipes or pop off elbows. This should not be too difficult to imagine since we deal with pipes in the house everyday.

This man was proudly showing me this irrigation system that he installed, and when he turned the valve on, the ground vibrated like crazy,, but he thought it was normal. Then the valve would about jump out of the ground with water hammer when he shut the whole mess off. I didn't want to tell him that his system was a mess and would need to be redone, because he was the type that would argue the point. He probably found out later when an elbow blew off and blasted high pressure water all over the garden for the full twenty minute timer cycle in the middle of the night. Needless to say, this type of phenomenon should be avoided in your yard.

The last fundamental point deals with normal pressure between 40 and 60 pounds per square inch. As each water outlet is added, then more water is called to move in the pipe, and more pressure is lost per foot of travel as each outlet is drilled. At first the water exceeds the safe speed limits, then finally so much pressure is lost that the water will barely trickle out the sprinkler or outlet. To prevent this, the pipe is gradually made larger from 3/4" starting size and usually ends at 1 1/4" that connects to the valve. In larger pipe, a smaller percentage of the particles are rubbing on the walls, and a limited number of outlets are installed so a minimum operating pressure is maintained. The main idea is avoiding too little or too much pressure at each head, and to have a water speed limit inside the pipe to avoid water hammer type tickets from the hydraulic cop!

Water pressure increases when going down hill and decreases while traveling up hill in a pressurized pipe. To determine pressure loss, figure for every foot rise in elevation, your system will lose .433 pounds per square inch of pressure. In ten feet of rise then 4.33 pounds will be lost which is not too awful. The point is to think about this when designing and hire a consultant when the yard has high hills and the pressure is minimal.

Well this is enough theory, so lets get into the nuts and bolts of irrigation.

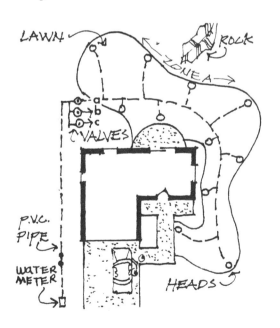

Irrigation begins at the water meter or well and ends with rain!

Getting Started: City water is usually supplied under pressure by a big pipe under the street called the 'water main' and your water comes off a copper pipe called the 'service line' that attaches to a water meter. The service line is usually the same size as the water meter that is usually one of three sizes for homes: 5/8", 3/4" or 1". So what? Well, the meter size, service line diameter, and the water pressure, measured in pounds per square inch or PSI, determines how many sprinkler heads you can have on one valve and line commonly called a 'zone' or curcuit. The water meter will allow so many gallons per minute or GPM's to pass through and the bigger the meter the more GPM's. We have covered all kinds of terms that we will use throughout this section.

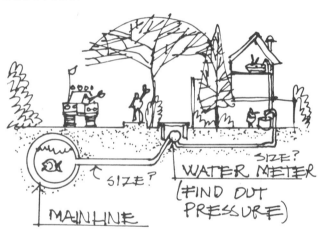

Find the water meter.

Call the city's water department and ask for your water meter size, the water pressure, and the service line size if they have it. You could measure the pressure with a gauge that attaches to a hose bib, read the meter size if it is visible, and measure the service line diameter but calling the city is easier and more accurate. Don't make any mistakes here, or the whole system will be screwed up.

If you are on a well, then determine the pressure and how many GPM's that can be pumped over a set time limit equal to a watering cycle. Some wells 'pump down' or go dry before the watering cycle is complete which is good to know before the system is installed! This oversight can botch up a good plan. Well logs, available in the water master's office of the county court house, usually have this information. If this information is not available, then measure the GPM's by filling a fifty gallon drum with pipe larger in diameter than the narrowest restriction and time it. If it takes 5 minutes to fill the drum then the well produces 10 gallons per minute. Measure the pressure with a pressure gauge and you are ready to design.

Now, use the following chart to determine how many GPM's that you can use per zone and from here on out this will be called your magic number. If each sprinkler head uses two GPM's and you string twenty heads on one zone, but the meter is only allowing twenty five GPM's through, then your system will have a few problems! Demanding 40 GPM's when 25 GPM's are available is a no, no, in irrigation just as overdrawing is a no, no, in banking.

"MAGIC NUMBER" CHART

How many heads or how many gallons per minute (g.p.m.'s) per zone?

SIZE OF:		STATIC PRESSURE POUNDS PER SQUARE INCH (P.S.I.)		
Pipe from main to Meter	Water Meter	Hire Consultant 45psi less	45	55	65
1/2"	5/8"				
3/4"	5/8"		6	7	8
3/4"	3/4"		8	10	11
1"	3/4"		10	13	15
3/4"	1"		13	16	18
1"	1"		10	13	15
			17	22	25

You should have your magic number or the number of GPM's that can be used and not exceeded per zone. This is important, so double check it.

Head Selection

Pick up a catalog on sprinkler heads at a store that carries irrigation supplies. Rainbird and Toro make irrigation supplies of excellent quality and we use lots of Toro heads. Rain Jet and Lawn Genie supply complete irrigation packages, that includes a design booklet with information on their heads. The idea is to use few heads, that will cover the yard which will reduce the amount of trenching and piping required. If the yard is 30' wide then use a 30' radius head for along the edge. For most homes, there are two kinds of heads that I will suggest. They are the pop up spray head, for short distances, made by Rain Bird, Toro, Rain Jet, and Lawn Genie, and the pop up gear driven head, for long distances, made by Toro or Hunter. Pop ups are out of sight, will not be broken off easily, and come in 3" and 4" heights for lawns and 6" and 12" for shrub beds. Certain tall ground covers may require heads on stand pipes. If the water source is from a well or irrigation canal where sand and debris get into the line, then impact heads are the best since they don't plug as easily.

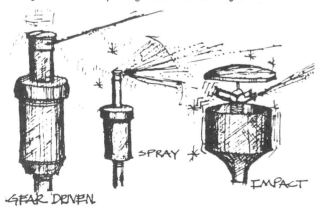

Here are the basic head types.

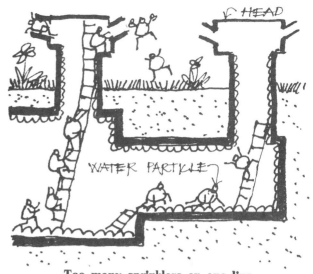

Too many sprinklers on one line won't work!

Most heads operate between 20 PSI and 50 PSI, and each head puts out a set number of GPM's, so look at this information on the charts. Choose heads that will require 70% or less of the starting pressure at the water meter. Take the starting water pressure and multipy it by .7 to determine the maximum pressure that can be expected at the far end of the system where the heads will be running. If you have 60 PSI at the water meter, then by the time the water particles have squeezed through the little meter hole, have rushed through the valves, and have run along the long relatively rough pipe, the pressure has dropped since the water particles have simply tuckered out! After this long journey, they have lost some of their driving energy needed to propell them through the sprinkler hole and out onto the plants. (60 PSI x .7 = 42 PSI or less for head pressure)

If your starting pressure is below 30 PSI, or the yard goes up high hills, or there are vast distances of pipe per zone like 400' or more, then you should hire an expert to help oversee your project or it might be a mess. If the head pressure is well above the maximum stated head pressure then install a device called a pressure reducer or the heads will mist rather than spray. Too much pressure can foul up a sprinkler system just as too little pressure can, so calculate the pressure carefully.

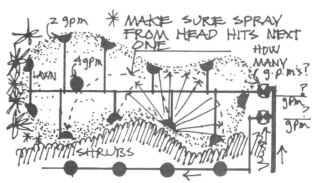

One line for lawns & one for shrubs.

Head Layout

Now pull out the landscape plan that should be accurate and to scale or you may end up watering the house, car, and neighbors patio! Find a compass for drawing circles and draw arcs that represent spray radiuses. Note that some heads can be adjusted to spray less than the maximum and some are not adjustable like some gear driven heads. Use quarter heads in corners, half heads along edges, and full heads for interior spaces. The spray from a head should go out far enough to hit all adjacent heads and this is called "head to head" coverage. Some people try to stretch heads by overlaping only the edge of the sprays and this is what causes the lawn to look like a leopard, with big dry spots among green lawn. Some people may want this abstract effect but most people want the leopards in the jungle. Water lawns and shrub beds separately and don't mix head types, like spray heads with gear driven heads because this causes effects that are worse than the spotted leopard effect on the lawn. Heavy watering heads will flood, while light watering heads are just getting the ground damp that causes interwoven green patches with dry grass areas. Sounds neat, doesn't it!

Zoning

Now that the heads are layed out begin to group compatible heads like the Toro 570 lawn heads and add the GPM's until your magic number is reached. (the maximum GPM's per zone that should have been figured as described earlier) Again group the lawns, shrub beds, and head types separately. For example, Toro makes two types of pop up spray heads, standard and low gallonage, and these should not be mixed on one zone. Quarters, halves, and full heads of one group can be mixed in a zone. Clear as mud? If this is confusing, then ask an expert in an irrigation supply store. Try to keep the zones all about the same number of GPM's. This is called balancing. Now connect the heads on one zone to pipe lines. When designing, avoid tree roots and rocky areas or you will be in for lots of digging and grubbing later. Run pipes well around trees and bedrock areas.

Avoid tree roots when trenching.

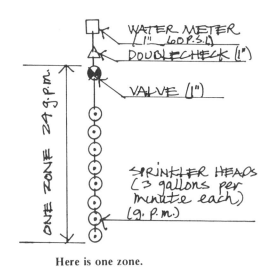

Here is one zone.

Valves & Vacuum Breakers

Locate vacuum breakers uphill from heads and after each valve or plan one doublecheck valve uphill or downhill from the heads and before the valves. Confused? These deals are known as backflow preventers and they keep standing water from getting sucked back into our drinking water. There have been cases when the main water line broke, flowed back downhill, created a suction, and pulled standing water with pesticides back in through low sprinkler heads. This could poison an entire neighborhood or town, so do this part right, since it is a state law for a reason. Granted, some of our law makers are a little screwed up at times, but this time they weren't. The doublecheck valve is expensive ($150 for a 1") but pays off with four or more valves.

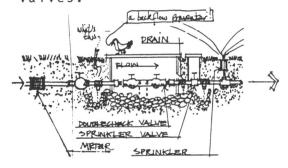

A doublecheck valve. (What's that?)

Locate manual valves in groups and close to the house so you won't have to wander all over the yard looking for buried valves. Use a 1" combination manual valve and vacuum breaker for most systems, since they are cheap and easy to install. However, if you are on a hillside then the vacuum breaker valve combination must be 15" above the highest head in order to work. Another method is to group 1" regular manual valves close to the house and to install a 1" doublecheck valve right after the water meter. The doublecheck valve can be installed below heads but vacuum breakers will not function if installed this way. Locate electric valves close to the zones and use a 1" doublecheck valve.

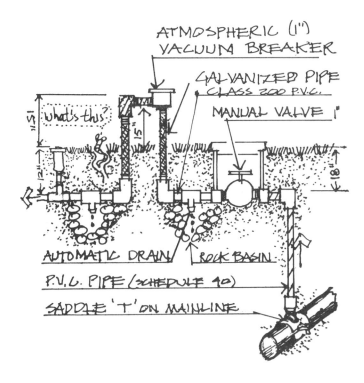

Starting at the mainline.

Timers

A timer should be located close to a 110 volt outlet where it can be plugged in and where wires can easily be run out through the wall, then underground to the valves. Some timers are for exterior wall locations while some are made for damp free interior locations. Place the timer where it is convenient to check and set, yet out of range for curious kids who may want to reprogram your watering cycles that took you an hour to figure out!

The computer timers are very flexible in terms of watering cycle options and they are generally less expensive than the old sturdy, wheel and gear type timers. For example, some computer timers can be set to turn on valves four times a day, which is important when establishing a new lawn. New lawns need to stay damp during hot weather or they will burn up, and four ten minute shots a day works great for germinating lawns. The old timers don't provide this option. However, some people who have trouble with programming find computer timers very frustrating and down right impossible to use. As a result of this, a combination computer and wheel timer has come out on the market that seems to be gaining popularity. Good reliable timers are made by Toro, Rainbird, Weathermatic, and Moody. A cheap timer may stick and cause a flood during the night, or it may not work during your two week vacation in August and will be the cause for the transformation of your lush garden into the Gobi Desert! Anyway, pick out a good timer since this is an important part of the irrigation system.

Pipe Sizing

The last head is on small pipe that gradually increases in size as we go towards the valve which helps prevent a radical pressure loss. Begin with 3/4" pipe at the last head on a zone, and total the head cumulative GPM's as you advance from head to head and change to 1" pipe when 10 GPM's is reached. Simple? Keep adding and change to 1 1/4" when 15 GPM's is reached and make sure that your

magic number is not exceeded when you arrive at the valve. Write each pipe size on the plan and you have it, good!

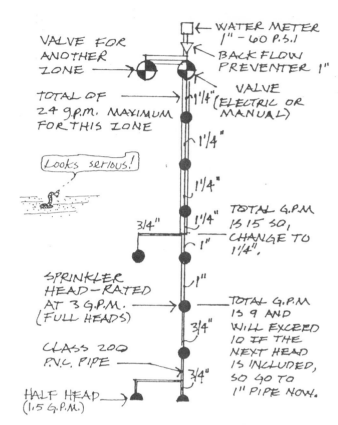

Start with 3/4" pipe at the last head, and gradually increase to 1¼". (simple!)

This concludes the irrigation design section and remember the goal is to water the shrubs and lawn and not the house! Plan out the whole system so each head will have enough pressure and use the right head for the right situation. Hire an irrigation contractor to check your plans if you are in doubt. Well, nice talking with you and have fun with the irrigation.

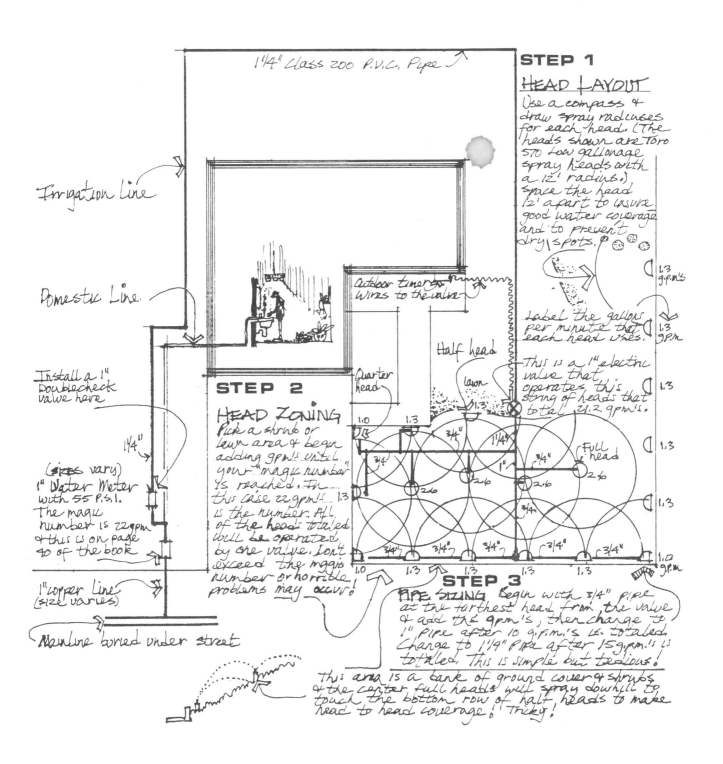

1'4" Class 200 P.V.C. Pipe

Irrigation Line

Domestic Line.

Install a 1"
Doublecheck
valve here

1'4"

(sizes vary)
1" Water Meter
with 55 P.S.I.
The magic
number is 22gpm
& this is on page
40 of the book

1" copper line
(size varies)

Mainline buried under street

STEP 1

HEAD LAYOUT
Use a compass &
draw spray radiuses
for each head. (The
heads shown are Toro
570 Low gallonage
spray heads with
a 12' radius.)
Space the head
12' apart to insure
good water coverage
and to prevent
dry spots.

Label the gallons
per minute that
each head uses.

This is a 1" electric
valve that
operates this
string of heads that
total 21.2 gpm's.

1.3 g.p.m's
1.3 g.p.m
1.3
1.3
1.3

Outdoor timer
wires to the valve

Half head

lawn
1.3

Quarter
head
1.0   1.3

STEP 2

HEAD ZONING
Pick a shrub or
lawn area & begin
adding gpm's until
your "magic number"
is reached. In
this case 22 gpm's
is the number. All
of the heads totaled
will be operated
by one valve. Don't
exceed the magic
number or horrible
problems may occur!

Full
head
2.6

3/4"
1"
3/4"
3/4"

2.6   2.6   2.6

3/4"
3/4"   3/4"   3/4"   3/4"   3/4"

1.0   1.3   1.3   1.3   1.3   1.0 g.p.m

STEP 3
PIPE SIZING Begin with 3/4" pipe
at the farthest head from the valve
& add the gpm's, then change to
1" pipe after 10 g.p.m's is totaled.
Change to 1'4" pipe after 15 g.p.m's is
totaled. This is simple but tedious!

This area is a bank of ground cover & shrubs
& the center full heads will spray downhill to
touch the bottom row of half heads to make
head to head coverage! Tricky!

Irrigation design for one zone.

chapter 5
PLANT CHARTS

The plant list on the following pages will help with the process of deciding on what plants are most suited for your landscape while madly designing or standing in the nursery among the myriads of plants with a blank look on your face. The plant charts were carefully prepared for your geographic location, now ask for the plant or find it and look it up. Most nurseries stock safe, hardy plants, so it would be wise to select plants from their selection by choosing a plant that closely matches the one you wanted or browse around the local nurseries and pick a few plants from each nursery.

In the northern geographic limits (Eugene, Oregon north) the plants will take more sun than what is shown on the plant charts. For example, rhododenrons in southern Oregon are grown in deep shade while they can be grown in the sun around the Portland, Oregon area. When applying the plant list to northern Pacific coastal areas, consult with the local nursery owners as to which plants will tolerate the direct burning wind and drying salt air. Now, the system used for the plant charts is simple and explained below, so learn to read the symbols rapidly. For example, f = filtered sun or morning sun. See--easy, so now pick the right plants for your yard situation, and plant, plant, plant!

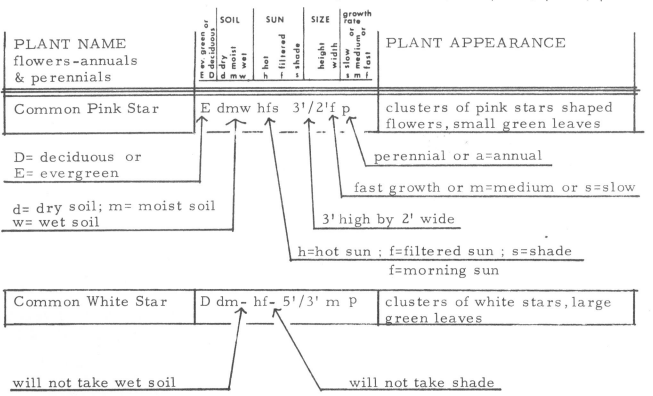

Ground Cover

Legend:
- SOIL: m ev. green or D deciduous; d dry, 3 moist, e wet
- SUN: x hot, - filtered, + shade
- SIZE: height, width; growth rate — s slow, 3 medium, f fast
- APPEARANCE / Botanical Name
- LEAF
- FLOWER / BERRY / BARK
- OTHER INFORMATION

Common Name	Type	Soil	Sun	Size	Growth	Appearance / Botanical Name	Leaf	Flower/Berry/Bark	Other Information
1) Ajuga or Carpet Bugle	E	-m-	hf-	6"/3'	m	green or purple dense mass, Ajuga reptans	2" rounded green	blue spikes, summer	purple and varigated varieties, neat plant for planters
2) Bearberry	E	dm-	hf-	3"/5'	m	trailing open, low shrub, green, Cotoneaster dammeri	1/2" d. green, oval, tough	red berries	neat rock garden plant
3) Broom, Kew	E	dm-	hf-	1'/4'	m	dark green, upright rods, dense, Cytisus kewensis	10" rods, d. green		rock gardens, dry planters
4) Ceanothus, Pointreyes	E	dm-	hf-	1'/8'	m	irregular, upright shoots, dense, green mass, Ceanothus gloriosa	3/4" serrated, tough d. green	blue puffy flowers, summer	good, massive cover for gardens
5) Hypericum, or Aaron's Beard St. John's Wart	E	-m-	-hf	1'/5'	f	lush green mass, upright limbs, neat, Hypericum calicinum	2" oval, green, summer	yellow flower, summer	spreads fast in good soil, will invade lawns, underground shoots
6) Ivy, Algerian	E	dmw	-fs	10"/15'f		regular mass, tropical looking, Hedera canariensis	8" lobed, gloss, green		vigorous cover, climbs, wedges under wood
7) Ivy, English	E	-m-	hfs	8"/10'	f	regular mass, neat looking, Hedera Helix	5" lobed, d. green		vigorous cover, climbs, wedges under wood, not hot sun
8) Juniper, Andorra Horizontal	E	dm-	hf-	1'/6'	m	gray-green mat, plum color in cold, upright shoots, Juniperus horizontalis 'plumosa'	juniper needles		neat for desert scenes, rock gardens
9) Juniper, Bar Harbor Horizontal	E	dm-	hf-	9"/5'	m	blue-gray mat, purple in winter, Juniperus horizontalis 'Bar Harbor'	juniper needles		neat for desert scenes, rock gardens
10) Juniper, Shore	E	dm-	hf-	9"/5'	m	irregular, upright, l. green mass, Juniperus conferta	1" long needles	light berries	neat for rough texture
11) Juniper, Waukegan Horizontal	E	dm-	hf-	9"/5'	m	steel gray mat, purple in winter, Juniperus horizontalis 'Douglasii'	juniper needles		neat for desert scenes, rock gardens
12) Juniper, Webber Horizontal	E	dm-	hf-	4"/5'	m	dense blue-green mat, Juniperus horizontalis 'Webberi'	juniper needles		retains color all year, desert scenes
13) Juniper, Wilton Horizontal	E	dm-	hf-	4"/5'	m	silver-blue tight mat, dense, Juniperus horizontalis 'Wiltonii'	juniper needles	gray berries	desert scenes, rock cascade
14) Kinninnick	E	dm-	hf-	8"/8'	m	open spreading mass, dense at times, dark green, Arctostaphylos uva-ursi	3/4" roundish, leather like, d. green		good planter cover in sun, native to Cascade Mountains
15) Moss, Irish	E	-m-	hf-	8"/8'	m	d. green, fine grasslike mat, Sagina subulata	hair-like fibers	tiny white flowers, summer	special ornamental garden plant, use around ponds, courtyards
16) Moss, Scotch	E	-m-	hf-	1"/12"	s	fine grasslike mat, yellow green, Sagina subulata 'Aurea'	hair-like fibers	tiny white flowers summer	same as above
17) Pachysandra, Japanese	E	-m-	-fs	8"/1'	m	green upright mass, Pachysandra terminalis	d. green 2" on top of stem	white flowers in summer	nice ground cover for planters
18) Periwinkle, Bigleaf	E	-m-	-fs	18"/10'f		irregular arching mass, thick, Vinca major	3", gloss, l. grn. summer	blue flowers, spring	nice for large areas, ragged, will take some sun
19) Periwinkle, Common	E	-m-	-fs	6"/5'	m	fine, arching, neat mass, Vinca minor	2", elongated, pointed	blue flowers, early spring	nice, shady garden plant
20) Potentilla, or Spring Cinquefoil	E	-m-	hf-	4"/2'	f	bright green, neat mat, dies back in the winter, Potentilla verna	1/2" roundish, lobed	tiny, massing, yellow flowers, all summer	nice for sunny planters, small areas

47

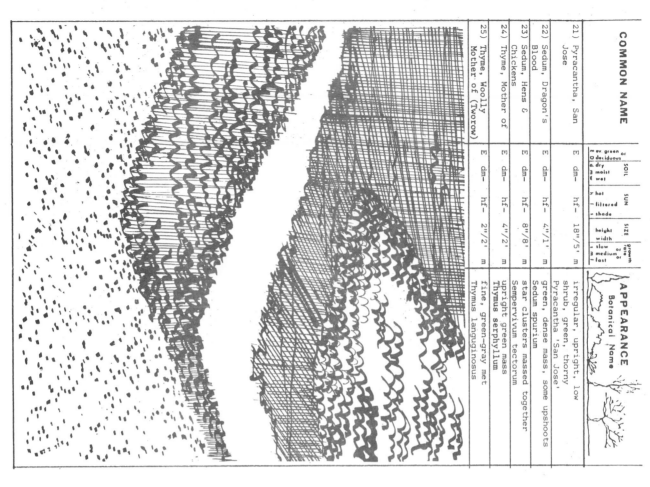

COMMON NAME	SOIL	SUN	SIZE (height/width)	growth rate	APPEARANCE / Botanical Name
21) Pyracantha, San Jose	E dm-	hf-	18"/5'	m	irregular, upright, low shrub, green, thorny / Pyracantha 'San Jose'
22) Sedum, Dragon's Blood	E dm-	hf-	4"/1'	m	green, dense mass, some upshoots / Sedum spurium
23) Sedum, Hens & Chickens	E dm-	hf-	8"/8'	m	star clusters massed together / Sempervivum tectorum
24) Thyme, Mother of	E dm-	hf-	4"/2'	m	upright green mass / Thymus serphyllum
25) Thyme, Woolly Mother of (Tworow)	E dm-	hf-	2"/2'	m	fine, green-gray met / Thymus languinosus

SOIL: E ev green / D deciduous, a dry, m moist, w wet. SUN: h hot, f filtered, s shade. growth rate: s slow, m medium, f fast.

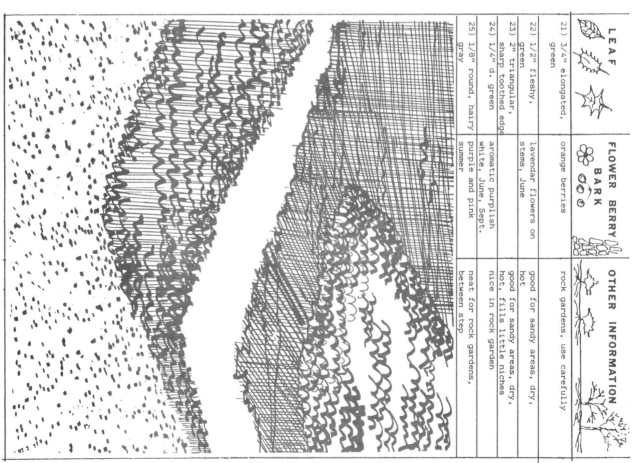

LEAF	FLOWER BERRY BARK	OTHER INFORMATION
21) 3/4" elongated, green	orange berries	rock gardens, use carefully
22) 1/2" fleshy, green	lavendar flowers on stems, June	good for sandy areas, dry, hot
23) 2" triangular, sharp toothed edge		good for sandy areas, dry, hot, fills little niches
24) 1/4" d. green	aromatic purplish white, June, Sept.	nice in rock garden
25) 1/8" round, hairy gray	purple and pink summer	neat for rock gardens, between step

COMMON NAME

(handwritten title:) Flowers

APPEARANCE — Botanical Name

Legend:
- m ev. green or / D deciduous
- SOIL: d dry / m moist / w wet
- SUN: h hot / f filtered / s shade
- SIZE: height / width
- growth: s slow or / m medium or / f fast

LEAF — FLOWER BERRY BARK — OTHER INFORMATION

#	Common Name	Ev/Dec	Soil	Sun	Size (h/w)	Growth	Appearance / Botanical Name	Leaf	Flower / Berry / Bark	Other Information
1	Aster, Oregon	D	-m-	h-	15"/15"	m	upright open plant / Aster hybridus	pointed oblong	2" blue, pink or white star-like l. summer	nice flowers for cutting perennial
2	Aubrieta, Common	E	dm-	hf-	6"/18"	m	low gray green mat / Aubrieta deltoides	small gray green leaves	rose to lavender flowers	rock gardens, shear blooms or they will seed all over, perennial
3	Balloon Flower	E	-m-	hf-	3'/2'	m		2" olive green leaves		nice show of color, foliage rough looking, perennial
4	Basket of Gold or Lamb's Ears	E	-m-	hf-	9"/1'	m	clumps of gray green foliage / Alyssum saxatile	2" elongated, hairy	dense gold clusters looking, early summer	beautiful, showy plant, garden border, perennial
5	Candytuft, Evergreen	E	-m-	hf-	1'/3'	m	neat, roundish green mass / Iberis sempervirens	1/4" elongated, l. green	profuse, long lived white flowers	
6	Carnation, Border	E	dm-	hf-	18"/2'	m	upright fine gray mass / Dianthus caryophyllus	2" gray green, hairy	2" orange, red, white yellow on tall stalks summer - fall	nice for planters or tubs, cut 'Rose Bowl' for variety, low mat, perennial
7	Christmas Rose	E	-m-	-fs	1'/1'	m	green clusters of leaves, low / Helleborus niger	5+ basal leaflets fans, green, 7-9 lobe	white flowers, stalks, winter	neat lushy garden plant, along paths, foresty, perennial
8	Common Thrift	E	dm-	hf-	6"/1'	m	grass-like tufts, green / Armeria Maritima	3" grass-like, green	flowers pink on stems spring and summer	nice accent plant, long blooms perennial - do well in poor, dry soil
9	Coneflower, Orange	D	-m-	hf-	2'/1'	m	nice bright flower / Rudbeckia fulgida	3" long, narrow pointed	3" yellow with dark center - l. summer	good plant for showy flower garden
10	Coral Bells	E	-m-	-f-	2'/8"	m	tall upright, airy / Heucheria sanguinea	2" roundish, bronze, scalloped	pink on 2' drooping stalks, April-August	native to Pacific coast, lush garden plant, waterfalls, perennial
11	Daisy, Shasta	D	-m-	hf-	18"/2'	f	upright green mass / Chrysanthemum maxima	elongated, rough green	2" white petals & gold center, summer, fall	hardy, dependable for flower garden perennial - need rich soil
12	Delphinium, Candle	D	-m-	hf-	5'/1'	f	tall long shoot / Delphinium elatum	basal, divided, green	flowers red, blue, long lasting-l. spring	acid soil stunts growth, needs rich soil, perennial
13	Dusty Miller	D	-m-	h-	2'/1'	m	neat silvery foliage - fernlike / Centaurea rutifolia	silvery, fernlike leaves	yellow or purple summer-fall flower	annual - noted for its neat foliage
14	English Lavendar	E	-m-	hf-	3'/3'	m	dense, upright, broom-like, gray / Lavandula spila	2" gray, narrow leaves	lavender, dense, spikes, mid summer	neat color and texture, desert type perennial
15	Foxglove, Common	D	-m-	hf-	4'/1'	f	tall long shoot / Digitalis purpurea	basal gray green hairy	white or purple flowers, May-Sept.	nice background flower garden plant, foresty, Pac Coast native, biennial
16	Lenten Rose	E	-m-	-fs	1'/1'	m	green clusters of leaves, low / Helleborus orientalis	5+ basal leaflets fans, green, 5-11 lobe	rose-purple flowers early spring, stalks	neat lushy garden plant, along paths foresty, perennial
17	Marigolds	D	-m-	hf-	9"/1'	m	upright green plant / Tagetes	2" basal, green	large double, orange spring-summer	nice brilliant flowers, borders, smell repells bugs, annual
18	Pansy	D	-m-	-f-	6"/1'	m	tufts of green / Viola wittrockiana	3" narrow lobed	3/4" white, other colors, spring-summer	annuals in some areas, flower garden perennial
19	Peony, Chinese	D	-m-	hf-	3'/3'	f	open, bushy look, green / Paeonia Lactiflora	large, d. green, divided	6" red, rose, salmon spring	neat garden plant, tuberous roots perennial
20	Phlox, Moss	E	-m-	hf-	6"/2'	m	neat low green mass / Phlox subulata	1/2" stiff, needle-like	white, rose, lavender, pink, late spring	neat rock garden plant, short bloom perennial
21	Primrose, Himalayan	D	-mw	hf-	8"/1'	m	tufts of green / Primula derticulata	bright green 4", long veined	2" lilac colored ball, spring	flower gardens, walk edges perennial - acid soil - boggy

Bulbs & Tubers

Legend — SOIL: ev. green or Deciduous; dry, moist, wet · SUN: hot, filtered, shade · SIZE: height/width; slow, medium, fast growth

# Common Name	Soil	Moisture	Sun	Size (h/w)	Growth	Appearance (Botanical Name)	Leaf	Flower · Berry · Bark	Other Information
1) Anemone, Poppy Flowered	D	-m-	hf-	9"/9"	m	irregular, showy flowers, fine texture – Anemone coronaria	finely divided green leaves	red-blue-white 2" x green leaves	neat for borders, rock gardens
2) Baboon flower	D	-m-	hf-	9"/9"	m	upright plant with sword leaves Babiana	18" stems – spring	blue-lav.-red-white tuberous	neat for path edges – rock
3) Bearded Iris	D	-m-	hf-	2'/1'	f	upright, sword-like leaves 1. green, Iris	3"/18" sword-like	all colors, spring-summer	gardens – corn
4) Berginia, Heartleaf	E		-fs	8"/1'	m	clump of big green leaves Berginia cordifolia	6" oval, green, wavy edges	long stalk, pink cluster stalks, e.sprg	nice for gardens, leaves are nice texture – variable height – tuber
5) Crocus	D	-m-	hfs	6"/6"	f	small green Crocus	long narrow, green	all colors except red	lush garden plant, paths, winter
6) Daffodils	D	-m-	hfs	6"/6"	f	upright thin green leaves Narcissus	1/2" x 10" green,	white petals & yellow cone center, spring	subtle garden plant – bulb
7) Dahlia	D	-m-	h--	15"+/15"+	m	large profuse showy flowers, height depends on variety Dahlia	oblong 2", m. green	3" star shape – all colors – summer	neat for flower gardens – bushy plant – tuber
8) Gladiolus	D	-m-	hf-	1'+/1'	f	upright, sword-like leaves, 1. green, Gladiolus	2"/1'+ sword-like long	all colors, summer	garden plant, some fall over due to height & wind – bulb
9) Hyacinth, Common	D	-m-	hf-	8"/8"	f	upright clumps Hyacinthus orientalis	green, upright, long	blue or white, dense spring	nice border plant – bulb
10) Lily, Belladonna	D		-f-	2'/2'	m	clumps of bold leaves Amaryllis belladonna	bold leaves	rosy pink flowers on 2' stalks – August	good in dry areas – any soil – bulb
11) Lily, Day	D	-m-	hfs	2'/1'	m	clumps of long, narrow green	24" long narrow green leaf	3" yellow, orange star shaped flower	variable height – bloom in spring and summer
12) Lily, Fragrant Plantia	D		-fs	1'/1'	m	dense perennial groundcover Hosta plantaginea	heart-shaped, lengthwise veins	1 1/2" lily-like white flower in 1. spring	spread all over shady areas – clump
13) Lily of the Nile	E	-m-	hf-	5'/4'	m	long arching pointed leaves Agapanthus orientalis	5" x 3" leaves	5" ball of white + blue on long stalks – summer	accent plant for entrances, pools, mounds – tuberous
14) Lily, Torch	D	-m-	hf-	3'/3'	f	clump of long narrow leaves Kniphofia uvaria	10" green, long	spikes, early spring orange	neat accent plant, bright – bulb
15) Lily-Turt, Big Blue	E	-mw	hf-	18"/1'	f	dense mass of long narrow green, Liriope muscari	grass-like leaves up to 2'	midsummer spikes of white or lavender flowers	spreads by rhizomes
16) Tiger Flower	D	-m-	-f-	2'/2'	f	upright sword leaves Tigridia pavonia	18" ribbed sword-like	3" orange, pink, yellow white or 12" stalk – mid summer	neat along forest paths or ponds – bulb
17) Tulips	D	-m-	hf-	1'/6"	f	upright Tulipa	wide curly green	all colors except blue spring-summer	nice showy flower – bulb
18) Watsonia	D	-m-	h--	3'/2'	m	upright swordlike leaves Watsonia pyramidata	1" x 2 1/2 sword leaves	3" rose clusters on 3' stems – spring	grows in winter corn plant – needs staking

50

Deciduous Trees

Legend:

- SOIL: m = ev. green or D = deciduous; d dry, 3 moist, w wet
- SUN: h hot, f filtered, s shade
- SIZE: height / width
- growth rate: s slow or 3 medium or f fast

COMMON NAME	D	Soil	Sun	Size (h/w)	Growth	APPEARANCE / Botanical Name	LEAF	FLOWER · BERRY · BARK	OTHER INFORMATION
1) Alder, Red	D	—mw	hf—	50'/20'	f	straight trunk, upright, green / Alnus rubrum	3" oval, serrated edges, green	yellow tassles in fall	will grow in standing water, neat
2) Ash, European	D	—m—	hf—	30'/20'	m	dense, oval, green / Sorbus acuparia	9-15 leaflets, 1 1/2" serrated	white spring flowers, juvenile gray bark	winter branch structure, neat
3) Ash, Modesto	D	—mw.	hfs	50'/30'	f	round head, green / Fraxinus velutina 'Modesto'	leaflets, oblong leaves, 1. green		fast shade, breaks in wind, soggy soil
4) Ash, Oregon White	D	—mw	hfs	70'/50'	f	upright, round head / Fraxinus oregona	leaflets, 3" oval	male and female flowers, big buds	grows in wet soil, native to Ore-Cal-Wash, fast shade
5) Aspen, Quaking	D	—mw	hf—	50'/20'	f	upright, short straight out branches, white bark / Populus tremuloides	3" heart-shaped, green	whitish bark	native to Ore-Cal-Wash, takes wet soil, flutters in wind, gets in pipes
6) Beech, European	D	—m—	hf—	60'/40'	m	broad cone, weeping branches / Fagus sylvatica	dark green, 3" oval, wavy, red in fall	smooth gray bark	neat varieties 'Weeping', 'Tricolor', 'Copper', surface roots, no salts
7) Birch, European White	D	—mw	hf—	40'/20'	m	tall, narrow, delicate, weeping branches / Betula pendula	2" diamond shape, dark green	white peely bark, dark clefts	picturesque white bark, soggy soil drips sticky fluid
8) Birch, Paper	D	—mw	hf—	40'/20'	f	tall, narrow, delicate, little, weeps a / Betula papyrifera	4" gloss green	creamy white bark, peels	same as above
9) Catalpa, Western	D	dm—	hf—	60'/50'	m	round headed, green / Catalpa bignonioides	9" heart-shaped, green	1' bean pods	hardy shade tree, bean pods messy in lawns, Common Catalpa smaller
10) Cherry, Autumn Flowering	D	—m—	hf—	25'/25'	m	bushy flat crown / Prunus cerasifera		white to pink in fall & winter	winter flowering ornamental
11) Cherry, Japanese Flowering	D	—m—	hf—	20'/15'	m	wide flat crown / Prunus serrulata		profuse flowers, white	many beautiful varieties like 'Shiro fugen', 'Kuanzon', profuse flowers
12) Elm, American	D	—m—	hf—	80'/80'	m	vase shaped / Ulmus americana	3" toothed, rough oval, yellow fall col	flaky bark	extensive roots, messy but hardy and good shade tree in right area
13) Elm, Chinese	D	—m—	hf—	60'/50'	f	arching vase shape / Ulmus parvifolia	2" oval, leathery green, toothed	sycamore-like bark	good fast shade tree
14) Elm, English	D	—m—	hf—	100'/100'	m	vase shaped / Ulmus procera	3" roundish, toothed, hold green in fall		extensive roots, messy, good hardy shade tree in right area
15) Elm, Siberian	D	dm—	hf—	50'/40'	m	upright, green / Ulmus pumila	2" oval green, smooth		good hardy wind break, not good in yard
16) Honeylocust	D	dm—	hf—	60'/50'	f	angular branching, round, thorny, green / Gleditsia triacanthos	leaflets, leaves oval green, 1/2" fall yellow	14" winter bean pods	desert shade tree, clean varieties without thorns or pods, soil tolerant
17) Hornbeam, American	D	dm—	hf—	30'/20'	m	round headed / Carpinus caroliniana	2" d. green, toothed, reddish fall color	smooth gray bark, 3" fruit clusters	small hardy shade tree, clean
18) Hornbeam, European	D	dm—	hf—	40'/20'	m	dense pyramid, broad with age / Carpinus betulus	3" d. green, toothed, yellow in fall	5" long fruit clusters	small hardy shade tree, upright varieties available

DECIDIOUS TREES

	LEAF	FLOWER BERRY BARK	OTHER INFORMATION	COMMON NAME	SOIL	SUN	SIZE height/width	APPEARANCE (Botanical Name)
19	fan leaflets 5-7, 8" toothed, green	ivory spring flowers	similar to Red Horsechestnut but larger, drops big nuts	19) Horsechestnut, Common	D -m-	hf-	60'/40' m	dense shade, green, rounded / Aesculus hippocastanum
20	5" heart-shaped, green	yellow-white flowers June-July	smaller, upright varieties available, street tree, Little Leaf Linden	20) Linden, American	D -m-	hf-	50'/25' m	straight trunk, narrow crown / Tilia americana
21	leaflets 7-19, green, 1 1/2"	deep grooved bark, white flower clusters	thorny branches, good desert shade tree, winter bean pods	21) Locust, Black	D dm-	hf-	75'/40' f	open, sparse branching, green / Robinia pseudoacacia
22	5" coarse, green oblong leaves	tulip-like flowers, white-pink	feature plant, showy	22) Magnolia, Saucer	D -m-	hf-	25'/25' m	spreading, many branches / Magnolia soulangiana
23		white strap-shaped petals, early spring	showy ornamental, courtyards	23) Magnolia, Star	D -m-	hf-	10'/20' m	spreading limbs, many branches / Magnolia robus stellata
24	3 lobes, 3", red fall color		neat garden plant, for shady court-yards, narrow walk	24) Maple, Amur	D -m-	-fs	20'/10' m	in shade tall, twisty, multi-trunked, picturesque, green, Acer ginala
25	3-5 pointed lobes, 10" yellow fall color	June seeds that twirl when they fall	native to Oregon river banks, dense shade, will take wet soil	25) Maple, Bigleaf	D -mw	-fs	95'/70' f	broad spreading, green, coarse / Acer macrophyllum
26	heart-shaped, 5", deep veins, red fall color	green striped bark with silver markings	nice small shade tree	26) Maple, David's	D -m-	hf-	35'/25' m	upright round, green / Acer davidii
27	5-9 lobes, 4" deep fall color	fine greenish bark	feature garden plant, neat varieties 'Bloodleaf', 'Threadleaf'	27) Maple, Japanese	D -m-	-fs	20'/18' s	round, delicate form, umbrella / Acer palmatum
28	5", 5 pointed lobes, good fall color	green-yellow spring flowers	nice shade varieties, 'Crimson King', 'Schweder' (purple), 'Columnare'	28) Maple, Norway	D -m-	hf-	60'/50' m	round head, straight trunk, green / Acer platanoides
29	3-5 blunt lobes, shiny green, nice fall color	dull red fruit, silvery bark when young	will take wet soil, has nice red twigs	29) Maple, Red	D -mw	hf-	40'/30' f	round head, red buds, light bark / Acer rubrum
30	5 sharp pointed lobes, 5", fair fall color	peeling or flaking bark	fast shade, may break in the wind	30) Maple, Silver	D -m-	hf-	80'/50' f	open, spreading, vase-shaped, green / Acer saccharinum
31	3-5 sharp lobes, 5", pale under		nice shade tree, good red-yellow fall color	31) Maple, Sugar	D -m-	hf-	60'/40' m	rounded compact crown, green / Acer saccharum
32	5 blunt lobes, 3" rough edges, fall color	greenish bark when young	neat tree for shady courtyards, narrow walk, native to Ore-Cal-Wash	32) Maple, Vine	D -mw	-fs	20'/10' m	in shade tall, twisty, multi-trunked, picturesque, Acer circinatum
33	5" d. green, shape varies, lobed		good desert tree, alkaline soil	33) Mulberry, White	D dm-	hf-	50'/40' s	dense, d. green, round head / Morus alba
34	4" deep lobes, sharp triple points	dark, grooved bark, small pointed acorns	native to Ore-Cal, grand form	34) Oak, California Black	D dm-	hf-	60'/40' m	upright, spreading, vase shape green, Quercus kelloggii
35	3-7 round lobes, 3", drop late		upright varieties available, interesting form	35) Oak, English	D -m-	hf-	90'/50' m	short trunk, pyramid form / Quercus robur
36	3-7 lobes, 7x3", pointed		deep roots, same as above	36) Oak, Northern Red	D -m-	hf-	90'/60' f	round top, green / Quercus rubra
37	4" elongated, rounded lobes	1" acorns, gray grooved bark	native to Ore-Cal-Wash, takes heat and dry soil	37) Oak, Oregon White	D dm-	hf-	50'/40' s	round head, curving branches when old, green, Quercus garyanna
38	similar to above, gloss d. green, red fall		will not take drought or alkaline soil, trees look neat in a row	38) Oak, Pin	D -m-	hf-	80'/30' m	tall, slender, straight trunk, lower branches sag / Quercus palustris
39	6" deep pointed lobes, 1. green, red fall		deep roots, good lawn or street tree similar to N. Red Oak in looks	39) Oak, Scarlet	D -m-	hf-	60'/40' m	open, rounded head / Quercus coccinea
40	8" maple-like leaf	light tan peely bark, winter seed balls	soil tolerant, hardy in city, nearly like American Planetree	40) Planetree, London or Sycamore	D dm-	hfs	80'/60' f	dense round head, coarse, green / Platanus acerifolia

Soil key: m ev green or D deciduous; d dry, m moist, w wet. Sun key: s hot, - filtered, = shade. Size key: height / width; slow or medium or fast.

DECIDIOUS TREES

COMMON NAME	m ev. green or D deciduous	SOIL (d dry, m moist, w wet)	SUN (h hot, f filtered, s shade)	SIZE height/width	growth rate (s slow, m medium, f fast)	APPEARANCE / Botanical Name	LEAF	FLOWER / BERRY / BARK	OTHER INFORMATION
41) Plum, Blireana	D	-m-	hf-	25'/20'	m	umbrella shape, delicate, purple / Prunus blireana	2" oblong, purple, bronze in summer	pink flowers in Feb. & April	nice small ornamental lawn tree
42) Plum, Thundercloud or Plum, Cherry	D	-m-	hf-	30'/25'	m	umbrella shape, delicate, d. green / Prunus cerasifera	2" oblong, d. green	white flowers	nice small ornamental lawn tree
43) Poplar, California or Black Cottonwood	D	-mw		hfs180'/100'	f	upright, rounded / Populus trichocarpa	3" triangular, gloss green	grooved gray bark	good fast shade, wet soil, breaks in wind, invades pipes
44) Poplar, Carolina	D	-mw		hfs180'/60'	f	upright, rounded head / Populus canadensis 'Eugenei'	4" triangular, serrated edge, gloss	grooved bark	good fast shade, wet soil, breaks in wind, invades pipes
45) Poplar, Lombardy Black	D	dmw		hfs100'/20'	f	upright column, branches point up / Populus nigra 'Italica'	4" green, yellow fall color		nice along driveways in a row, not good in the lawn
46) Poplar, White	D	dmw		hfs 50'/50'	f	round head / Populus alba	3-5 lobes, 5"	white bark and dark flutters in wind	good desert plant, invades pipes, good in the lawn
47) Silktree	D	dm-	hf-	30'/30'	m	umbrella-shaped, fine texture green, / Albezzia julibrissan	fan-like leaflets, 1/4" oval green leaves	pink summer flowers at base	good in dry areas, neat courtyard tree, leaves leave stems
48) Smoke Tree	D	dm-	hf-	25'/10'	m	urn-shaped, sometimes shrub-like / Cotinus coggygria	2" roundish, blue green, yellow fall	lavender puffy flowers / smooth bark	likes dry soil, picturesque, purple leaf varieties available
49) Sweetgum, American	D	-m-	hf-	60'/30'	m	upright, rigis, straight trunk / Liquidamber styraciflua	5-7 pointed lobes	purple leaf varieties available	nice lawn tree, likes acid soil, brilliant orange fall color
50) Tuliptree	D	-m-	hf-	80'/40'	f	upright, straight trunk / Liriodendron tulipifera	6", rounded with two outward, pointed lobes	tulip-shaped yellow spring flowers	spreading roots, neutral to acid soil, interesting tree
51) Walnut, Black	D	-m-	hf-	100'/80'	m	round crown, vase-shaped, open / Juglans nigra	15+ leaflets, 3" oblong, green	grooved, black bark, hard shelled nut	stunts shrub growth under it like Rhodes' and Azaleas
52) Walnut, Persian or English	D	-m-	hf-	60'/60'	m	round head / Juglans regia	5+ leaflets, 5" oblong, green	smooth gray bark, big, good walnuts	usually grafted to Black Walnut root graft sometimes fails after 10 years

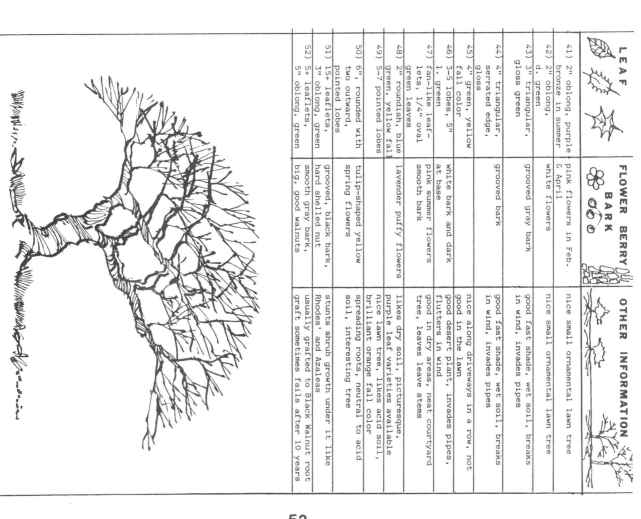

Legend

- E = ev. green or D = deciduous
- SOIL: d = dry, m = moist, w = wet
- SUN: h = hot, – = filtered, – = shade
- SIZE: height / width
- growth rate: s = slow, m = medium, f = fast

#	COMMON NAME	SOIL	SUN	height/width	growth	APPEARANCE (Botanical Name)	NEEDLES	CONE / BARK	OTHER INFORMATION
1	Arborvitae, American	E	—mw	hf—	60'/30'		upright, open branches turn up, yellow green, Thuja occidentalis	flat scales, yellow-green	erect cones with over-lapping scales	varieties more common, wet soil, Japanese varieties
2	Arborvitae, Oriental	E	—mw	hf—	30'/30'	m	shrubby, round foliage, Thuja orientalis	flat scale-like lapping scales	open 1/2" ball with hooked arms	ornamental tree, damaged in cold winds
3	Cedar, Atlas	E	dm—	hf—	80'/55'	s	horizontal branches, rigid, pyramid green, Cedrus atlantica	1" needle, stiff green w/blue needles		magnificent tree, blue variety
4	Cedar, Deodar	E	dm—	hf—	80'/40'	f	1. green, feathery, drooping, pyramid, Cedrus deodara	1/2", 1. green soft needle		
5	Cedar, Incense	E	dm—	hf—	80'/40'	m	drooping, soft, d. green, pyramid Libocedrus decurrens	flat, opposite scales, that split into wings		native to Cal-Ore-Wash, takes hot dry conditions
6	Cedar, Port Orford	E	—m—	hf—	60'/30'	m	dense, d. green, drooping, pyramid Chamaecyparis lawsoniana	flat scales, gloss, green	3/4" cones that open	dense screen when young, neat with other confiers
7	Cedar, Western Red	E	dm—	hf—	125'/100'	m	drooping, d. green, pyramid Thuja plicata	flat scales, green w/white	3/4" cones that open with petal-like scales	needs moisture, gold and erect varieties
8	Cypress, Hinoki False	E	dm—	hf—	40'/20'	m	d. green, open, spreading, flat fronds, Chamaecyparis obtusa	flat d. green scales		rock gardens, neat, upright, compact varieties
9	Cypress, Sawara False	E	dm—	hf—	20'/20'	m	green, round, open Chamaecyparis pisifera	spine-tipped scales		rock gardens, neat varieties, 'Plumosa', 'Threadleaf'
10	Fir, Douglas	E	dm—	hf—	120'/60'	m	d. green, open Pseudotsuga taxifolia	2" green needles point in all directions	2" feathered, red-brown cones	native to Pacific states
11	Fir, Grand	E	dm—	hfs	150'/60'	m	green, conical, lower drooping branches, Abies grandis	1 1/2" blunt, yellow-green opposite	3" erect, yellow-green cones	native to Pacific states, does best near the coast
12	Fir, Noble	E	dm—	hfs	150'/60'	m	blue-green, stiff, regular Abies procera	1 1/2" stiff, blue-green, sharp, up pointing	5" erect, feathered, yellow-green cones	native to Pacific states
13	Fir, White	E	dm—	hfs	150'/60'	m	d. green, uniform, slight droop Abies concolor	2" flat, opposite needles	4" erect, yellow-green cone	native to Pacific states, soft texture
14	Hemlock, Pacific	E	—m—	hfs	125'/50'	m	upright, pyramid, d. green, fine texture, Tsuga canadensis	3/4" gloss, soft, d. green, opposite needles	1" soft papery cones	native to foresty garden plant, needs room
15	Pine, Austrian	E	dm—	hf—	40'/30'	s	dense, uniform, stout, d. green Pinus nigra	3" stiff, d. green needle	3" oval, brown cone	takes cold, strong appearance, hardy
16	Pine, Bishop	E	dm—	hf—	40'/30'	s	open, pyramid when juvenile Pinus muricata	2's – 5" d. green	2" cones in whorls of 3	hardy, takes wind and salt
17	Pine, Eastern White	E	dm—	hf—	100'/50'	s	symmetrical, conical, green with blue tint, Pinus strobus	5's – 3" green with blue tint needle	5" slender cones, curved	hardy, burns in wind, fine texture
18	Pine, Japanese Black	E	dm—	hf—	80'/60'	f	irregular when young, d. green Pinus thunbergii	2's – 2" stiff, d. green needle	2" gray-brown cone	common garden plant, dense screen
19	Pine, Japanese Red	E	dm—	hf—	80'/60'	f	multi-trunked at times, picturesque form, open, Pinus densiflora	2's – 4" green needle	2" oval, brownish cone	neat in rock gardens, neat form

CONIFEROUS TREES

Legend:
- Botanical Name: ev green / deciduous
- SOIL: dry / moist / wet
- SUN: hot / filtered / shade
- SIZE: height / width
- growth rate: slow / medium / fast

No.	COMMON NAME	Type	Soil	Sun	Size (h/w)	Rate	APPEARANCE / Botanical Name	NEEDLES	CONE	BARK	OTHER INFORMATION
20)	Pine, Monterrey	E	dm-	hf-	80'/60'	f	broad cone when young, green / Pinus radiata	3's or 2's - 5" d. green needle	4" clustered, lopsided cones		dense screen when young, burns in cold winds and suffers in smog
21)	Pine, Ponderosa	E	dm-	hf-	150'/70'	m	upright, open, coarse, green / Pinus ponderosa	3's - 8" green needle	5" prickly, red brown	reddish bark	native to Pacific states, dry land tree, dense when young
22)	Pine, Scotch	E	dm-	hf-	70'/50'	m	dense, blue-green / Pinus sylvestris	2's - 2" stiff, blue-green needle	2" gray-red-brown cone	reddish bark	nice color with d. green pines, burns in cold wind,
23)	Pine, Shore	E	dm-	hf-	30'/20'	f	irregular and bent along coast, straight inland, d. green / Pinus conferta	2's - 1 1/2" d. green stiff needle	1 1/2" cone, yellow brown		nice small garden plant, contorts along the coast
24)	Pine, Swiss Mountain	E	dm-	hf-	15'/15'	m	multi-trunks, bushy, d. green / Pinus mugo	2's - 2" d. green needle	1 1/2" cones, oval, dark brown		hardy, sold as Mugho Pine by mistake, nice screen
25)	Pine, Tanyosho	E	dm-	hf-	20'/20'	s	low, round, bushy, d. green / Pinus densiflora 'Umbraculifera'	2's - 1" d. green needle	2" cones, roundish, light brown		hardy, neat for rock gardens
26)	Pine, Western White	E	dm-	hf-	60'/30'	f	fine texture, open, narrow blue-green, Pinus monticola	5's - 3" green w/blue tine, needle	8" cone, slender, light brown		native to Pacific states, hardy, gets blister rust
27)	Redwood, Coast	E	-m-	hfs	200'/100'	m	cone-shaped, fine texture, d. green / Sequoia sempervirens	prickly scale-like needles	1/2" cones		needs water, iron in the soil, lots of room, prickly texture
28)	Redwood, Giant	E	dm-	hfs	200'/100'	m	cone-shaped, d. green, prickly / Sequoia gigantea	1/2" soft, flat, pointed opposite needle	1/2" cones, terminal	blunt arms	needs water, room to grow
29)	Spruce, Colorado	E	dm-	hf-	100'/60'	m	dense, upright, l. green, rigid / Picea pungens	2" green, stiff, prickly needle	3" light brown, hanging cone		typical lawn ornament, neat varieties: 'Blue', 'Weeping', etc.
30)	Spruce, Norway	E	-m-	hf-	150'/80'	f	upright, pyramid, dense, d. green, drooping branches, Picea abies	1" d. green, prickly, bent needle	2" green,		cold area windbreak, many varieties
31)	Spruce, Sitka	E	-m-	hf-	150'/80'	m	rigid, pyramid, horizontal, green with blue tine, Picea sitkatensis	2" prickly, stiff needle	2" purplish, terminal cones		needs water and a moist atmosphere neat with other conifers

Broadleaf Evergreen

Legend — APPEARANCE / Botanical Name

- m ev. green or D deciduous
- SOIL: d. dry / m moist / w wet
- SUN: h hot / – filtered / + shade
- SIZE: height / width
- growth rate: s slow / m medium / f fast

COMMON NAME	(ev/dec)	SOIL	SUN	SIZE (h/w)	growth	APPEARANCE / Botanical Name	FLOWER BERRY BARK	LEAF	OTHER INFORMATION
1) Laurel, English	E	dm–	hf–	20'/20'	m	multi-trunked, rounded, green, dense, Prunus laurocerasus	dark berries, soft, 1/2"	4" gloss, green, oblong	usually a hedge, but prune to a tree
2) Laurel, Grecian or Sweet Bay	E	–m–	–f–	30'/20'	m	multi-trunked, compact, cone, d. green, Laurus nobilis	yellow flowers, dark purple berries	3" d. green leathery, aromatic	source of bay leaf spices, neat tree
3) Laurel, Portugal	E	dm–	hf–	20'/20'	m	dense, d. green, rounded, Prunus lusitanica	smooth gray bark	3" d. green, rough edge	usually a hedge, but prune to a tree
4) Madrone, Pacific	E	dm–	hf–	50'/30'	s	bending trunk, irregular, green, Arbutus menziesii	red berry clusters, reddish-tan peely bark	4" gloss, green, oblong	native to Pacific states, pretty bark, dry soil
5) Magnolia, Southern	E	–m–	–f–	80'/40'	m	upright, dense, rounded, green, Magnolia grandiflora	10" white flowers, summer-fall	6" glossy, oblong	lawn or street tree, smaller variety 'St. Mary'
6) Myrtle, Oregon or California/laurel	E	–m–	–f–	75'/100'	m	dense, spreading, green, Umbellularia californica	sparse flowers, purple nuts	4" gloss green, pointed, narrow	screen tree, aromatic leaf
7) Myrtle, Pacific Wax	E	–m–	–f–	30'/30'	m	multi-trunked, fine, green, Myrica californica		3" gloss, d. green, toothed	neat, fine texture, screen tree
8) Oak, Canyon Live	E	dm–	hf–	50'/40'	m	round headed, spreading, green, Quercus chrysolepis	smooth white bark, golden fuzzy acorns	1 1/2" green, oval, toothed or straight	native to Cal-Ore, rare in nurseries
9) Oak, Coast Live	E	dm–	hf–	60'/60'	m	round headed, dense, green, Quercus agrifolia	smooth gray bark	2" holly-like, green, gloss	nice street tree, greedy roots
10) Palm, Windmill	E	–m–	hf–	30'/10'	m	upright, green, palm tree, Trachycarpus fortunei		3' palm leaves, green	tropical foliage, neat in courtyards
11) Photinia, Chinese	E	dm–	hf–	35'/20'	m	upright, curving, green, Photinia serrulata	profuse white flowers in April-May	8" green, rough edges	prune to be a tree or will be bushy, gets mildew

Small to Medium Shrubs

COMMON NAME	SOIL	SUN	SIZE (height/width)	growth rate	APPEARANCE / Botanical Name	LEAF	FLOWER BERRY BARK	OTHER INFORMATION
1) Arborvitae, Dwarf Golden Oriental	E	-m-	5'/3'	m	green-gold globe Thuja orientalis 'Aurea'	green-gold scales		rock gardens, planters
2) Arborvitae, Globe American	E	-m:s	3'/5'	m	dense, green globe Thuja occidentalis 'Globosa'	green scales		rock gardens, planters
3) Azalea, Mollis	D	-m-	4'/4'	m	upright, green Rhododendron molle	nice fall color	red to yellow in May	nice middle ground plant, planters
4) Barberry, Chenault	E	dm-	4'/6'	s	low arching, d. green, spiny Berberis chenaulti	1" d. green, spiny, toothed	yellow flowers, May	low thorny barrier
5) Barberry, Japanese	D	dm-	6'/6'	m	arching vase, green, spiny Berberis thunbergi	3/4" tear drop shape, red in cold	red berries in fall-winter, Ma; ellow flowers	neat red leaf variety, nice little showy plant, barriers
6) Barberry, Rosemary	E	dm-	9'/4'	m	upright, arching, d. green, spiny Berberis stenophylla	3/4" inrolled, spiny, narrow, d. green	ora ed bright berries v:llow May flowers	nice barrier or screen
7) Barberry, Warty	E	dm-	3'/3'	m	d. green, spiny ball Berberis verruculosa	1" d. green, gloss, spiny, leather...	yellow May flowers	low thorny barrier red fall color
8) Broom, Warminster or Moonlight Broom	E	dm-	5'/6'	m	dense, d. green, mound, mass or long rod-like leaves, Cystisus praecox	10' r d-like leaves, d. green	profuse pale-yellow in March-April	desert plant, low mat variety, 'Kew Broom'
9) Candytuft, Evergreen	E	-m-	1/4'	m	green, spreading mound Iberis Sempervirens	tiny green leaves oblong	profuse white flowers spring	nice showy border plant
10) Cypress, Birds Nest	E	dm-	5'/5'	m	green, flat ball, conifer Chamaecyparis nidifera	d. green, soft needles		nice rock garden plant
11) Cypress, Dwarf Hinoki	E	dm-	4'/3'	m	dense foliage flat sided sprays Chamaecyparis obtusa 'Nana Aurea'	flat yellowish scales		nice for rock gardens
12) Daphne, Winter	E	-m-	4'/6'	m	lush, green, mound Daphne odora	3" oblong, green, gloss yellow edges	fragrant, pink Feb-March	temperamental, nice garden plant, needs right soil
13) Fern, Deer	E	-m-	1/2'	m	d. gloss green, fern leaves, upright Blechnum spicant	1" d. green fern leaves		native to Northwest, grows on ground and from trees, needs moisture
14) Fern, Western Sword	E	-m-	2/3'	m	green, fern leaves, upright, bunch of arching leaves Polystichum munitum	2' green fern leaf		native to Pacific states, accent plant, courtyards, or plant in bunch
15) Fern, Woodwardia	E	-m-	5'/6'	m	l. green, arching bunch of fern leaves, soft, Woodwardia fimbrata	5' light green, fern leaf		neat, shady garden plant, must stay moist, can grow to 9'
16) Fescue, Blue	E	dm-	1'/1'	m	blue-gray tufts of grass, whitish on top, Festuca ovina 'Glauca'	8" blue-gray grass-like leaf	tassles and seeds	little ornamental plant, needs good drainage, is not a ground cover
17) Heath, Spring	E	dm-	1/2'	m	upright pointing needles on limbs fine texture, d. green Erica carnea	d. green tiny	white or pink in spring & summer, long time	rock gardens, planters, paths, desert
18) Heather, Scotch	E	d:-	2'/2'	m	upright, yellow-green, fine needle-like, Calluna vulgaris	yellow-green needles	white flowers summer	nice for rock gardens, planters
19) Holly, Convexleaf Japanese	E	-m-	4'/5'	m	regular, green roundish Ilex crenata 'Convexleaf'	1/2" round, green curls to underside		nice shady garden plant, acid soil
20) Holly, Dazzler Chinese	E	-m-	2'/2'	m	dense, prickly, green ball Ilex cornuta 'Dazzler'	nice show of red berries		planters, low barriers, many other varieties 'Rotunda' 'Burfordii Nana'

Legend:
SOIL: m ev green or / D deciduous / d dry / m moist / w wet
SUN: h hot / - filtered / - shade
SIZE: height / width
growth rate: s slow / m medium / f fast

COMMON NAME	SOIL (ev. green/deciduous)	SOIL (dry/moist/wet)	SUN (hot/filtered/shade)	SIZE (height/width)	growth rate	APPEARANCE / Botanical Name	LEAF	FLOWER BERRY BARK	OTHER INFORMATION
21) Holly, Green Island Japanese	E	-m-	-fs	1'/2'	m	spreading, green, fine / Ilex crenata 'Green Island'	1/2" oblong, green	white flowers June, blue berries	nice shady garden plant, acid soil
22) Honeysuckle, Box	E	-m-	-fs	6'/5'	m	upright, bushy, d. green / Lonicera nutida	1/2" d. green gloss	white flowers in May, purple berries	shady middle ground plant
23) Honeysuckle, Privet	E	-m-	-fs	3'/5'	m	low, spreading, green mass / Lonicera nitida	1/2" d. green oblong		foresty, bank cover
24) Juniper, Phitzer Chinese	E	dm-	-fs	5'/15'	m	star-shaped, spreading, green / Juniperus chinensis 'Phitzer'	green, oblong		neat shape, barrier, varieties: 'Gold' 'Old Gold' (sm) 'Mint Julip' (upright green vase)
25) Juniper, Tam	E	dm-	hf-	10'/10'	m	bunching, upright green, mound / Juniperus sabina 'Tamariscifolia'	dull green, prickly needles		common shrub but tricky to use due to end result, prune to tree form
26) Mahonia, Cascades	E	dm-	-fs	2'/2'	m	green umbrella, foliage from top of stem, Mahonia nervosa	leaflets, prickly needles	yellow flowers April-June, blue berries	nice shrub middle ground plant, forest accent plant, paths
27) Nandina or Heavenly Bamboo	E	-m-	-fs	8'/4'	m	upright, umbrella, green-red / Nandina domestica	2" oblong, red new growth	whitish flowers spring	nice middle ground plant, small varieties, not a bamboo, Barberry
28) Oregon Grape Compact	E	-m-	hf-	1'/1'	m	loose, umbrella, fine / Mahonia aquifolium 'Compacta'	2" reddish-green holly-like	yellow summer flowers	dry land, nice foreground
29) Peony, Tree	D	-m-	-f-	6'/6'	m	open, neat branching, blue-green / Paeonia suffruticosa	large divided, bronze new gro.	large red-pink-lavender flowers, spring	nice garden plant, big flowers protect from wind, good drainage
30) Potentilla, Shrubby	D	dm-	hf-	2'/3'	m	open, spreading, green, twiggy / Potentilla fruticosa	small, lobed, green	1/2" yellow, June-October	hardy desert plant, need to blend with other plants due to sparse foliage
31) Raphiolepsis	E	dm-	hf-	6'/6'	m	flat, dense, d. green, ball / Raphiolepsis indica	2" leathery, d. green oblong	blackish berries May pink flowers	dry land plant, plant in bunches
32) Rhododendron, Blue Tit	E	-m-	hfs	3'/3'	m	green, roundish, fine / Rhododendron keiskei 'Blue Tit'	small, oblong, green	blue flowers in April	will take some sun, nice in garden or planter, 'Blue Diamond' similar
33) Rhododendron, Bow Bells	E	-m-	-s	4'/4'	m	rounded, green / Rhododendron augustinii 'Bow Bells'	2" rounded, green bronze new foliage	pink flowers in May	nice lush garden plant, courtyard
34) Rhododendron, Cilpinese Chryseum	E	-m-	-s	2'/5'	m	low spreading, fine texture / Rhododendron chryseum 'Cilpinese'	small green leaves	pinkish in March	lush garden plant, plant in masses
35) Rhododendron, Impeditum	E	-m-	-s	1'/1'	m	dense, gray-green, twiggy / Rhododendron impeditum	tiny gray-green leaves	d. blue flowers in April	will take some sun, needs good drainage, nice garden plant, planters
36) Rhododendron, Loder's White Keiskei	E	-m-	-s	5'/5'	m	neat, roundish, green / Rhododendron keiskei 'Loder's White'		pink or white in May	nice lush garden plant
37) Rhododendron, Moonstone	E	-m-	-s	2'/2'	m	round, dense, green, fine texture / Rhododendron macrophyllum 'Moonstone'	small rounded, green	pink-cream in April	nice lush garden plant
38) Rhododendron, Moupinese	E	-m-	-s	2'/2'	m	open, spreading, green / Rhododendron moupinese	1 1/2" oval, green, red new growth	white or pink Feb.-March	nice lush garden plant
39) Rhododendron, Mucronulatim	E	-m-	-s	5'/5'	m	spreading, open, green / Rhododendron, Korean	large hairy leaves	white-green flowers March-April	nice lush garden plant, is an Azalea
40) Rosemary	E	-m-	hf-	4'/4'	m	dense, irregular, upright, green / Rosemarinus officinalis	d. green, 1/2" puffy, narrow, blunt, fragrant	fall-winter-spring blue-lavender flowers	nice low variety that cascades, herb for cooking, nice flowers, low
41) Salal	E	dm-	hf-	5'/5'	m	green, stiff mound, spreading / Gaultheria Shallon	3" oval, leathery		native to coast, tall ground cover, takes salt air, sandy soil
42) Spruce, Nest	E	dm-	hf-	3'/5'	m	green, spreading, conifer / Picea abies 'Nest'	d. green needles, 1"		nice rock garden plant

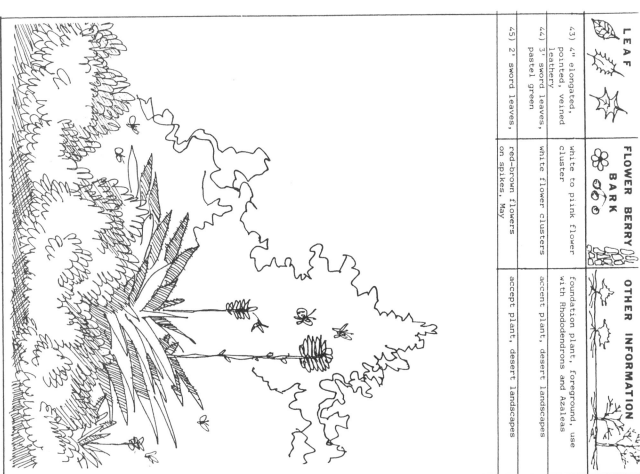

COMMON NAME	SOIL	SUN	SIZE	growth rate	APPEARANCE — Botanical Name
	m ev green or / □ deciduous / a dry / ɜ moist / ɛ wet	ɔ hot / - filtered / ⊙ shade	height / width	- slow / ɜ medium or / - fast	
43) Viburnum, David's	E	-m-	-fs	3/5'	m	dense, d. green, compact, coarse Viburnum davidi
44) Yucca, Adam's Needle	E	dm-	hf-	6'/6'	m	pastel green, bunch of up pointing sword leaves from the ground Yucca Filmentosa
45) Yucca, Dactil	E	dm-	hf-	3/3'	m	sword leaves on stem end, 1. green Yucca baccata

LEAF	FLOWER BERRY BARK	OTHER INFORMATION
43) 4" elongated, pointed, veined leathery	white to piink flower cluster	foundation plant, foreground, use with Rhododendrons and Azaleas
44) 3' sword leaves, pastel green	white flower clusters	accent plant, desert landscapes
45) 2' sword leaves,	red-brown flowers on spikes, May	accept plant, desert landscapes

Large Shrubs

COMMON NAME

SOIL: E ev. green or D deciduous · d dry · m moist · w wet
SUN: x hot · - filtered · = shade
SIZE: height / width / growth rate (s slow · m medium · f fast)
APPEARANCE · **LEAF** · **FLOWER · BERRY · BARK** · **OTHER INFORMATION (Botanical Name)**

#	COMMON NAME	SOIL	SUN	SIZE	APPEARANCE	LEAF	FLOWER/BERRY/BARK	OTHER INFORMATION (Botanical Name)
1	Abelia, 'Edward Goucher'	E/D -m-	hf-	6'/6' m	arching green mound, fine	oblong, green	pink in June-Oct.	Abelia hybrid-grandiflora/schumanni, showy, middleground, may grow to 5'
2	Abelia, Glossy	E -m-	hf-	8'/5' m	arching mound, green, fine	3/4" gloss, l. green, oval	white-pink June-Oct., showy, middleground	Abelia grandiflora, nice bank cover
3	Aralia, Japanese or Fatsia	E -m-	-fs	8'/6' m	dense, tropical look, green	16" maple-like, gloss, green	white flowers in fall-winter	Fatsia japonica, neat in courtyards, tropical foliage, coarse texture
4	Arborvitae, 'Beverly Hills' Oriental	E dm-	hf-	10'/10' m	upright cone, gold-green	gold-green flat scales	1/2" hooked arm cones	Thuja orientalis 'Beverly Hills' takes drier conditions, screen
5	Arborvitae, Pyramid American	E -m-	hf-	25'/5' m	dense green, upright column	green flat scales		Thuja occidentalis 'Pyramidalis' screen, needs moisture, screen
6	Arborvitae, Woodwardi Amer.	E -m-	hf-	8'/18' s	rich green globe, spreading	green flat scales		Thuja occidentalis 'Woodwardii' usually small, needs moisture
7	Azalea, Chinese	D -m-	-f-	6'/6' m	upright, green	orange fall color	yellow-orange in April	Rhododendron molle, showy garden
8	Azalea, Japanese	D -m-	-f-	6'/6' m	upright, green		salmon-red-orange in May	Rhododendron japonicum, showy garden plant
9	Azalea, Royal	D -m-	-fs	8'/8' m	upright, green	leaves in whorls - 5 at branch tip	pink flowers in April-May	Rhododendron schlippenbachii, protect from sun, showy pink
10	Azalea, Western	D -m-	-fs	8'/8' m	densely branched, green	small, roundish green	white-pink in May	Rhododendron occidentale, native to Northwest
11	Bamboo, Black	E -m-	hfs	8'/4' m	erect, green	1 1/2" green, oblong, pointed		Phyllostachys nigra, running, black stems, nice in tubs
12	Bamboo, Giant Timber	E -m-	hfs	35'/35' f	huge, tall, green	green		Phyllostachys bambusoides, running, needs lots of room or plant in tubs
13	Bamboo, Golden	E -m-	hfs	10'/10' m	erect, green, long stems	green, oblong, pointed		Phyllostachys aurea, running, tall screen
14	Bamboo, Hedge	E -m-	hfs	10'/10' m	erect, green, long stems	green		Phyllostachys multiplex, clump or does not run, nice in gardens
15	Barberry, Darwin	E dm-	hf-	8'/6' m	fountain-like, d. green	1" holly-like, d. green	orange flowers spring, dense, showy	Berberis darwinii, prickly screen
16	Barberry, Mentor	E dm-	hf-	7'/7' m	dense, compact, d. green	1" long, d. green		Berberis mentorensis, takes dry conditions, hedge
17	Barberry, Wilson	E dm-	hf-	6'/6' m	light green, ball, dense	3/4"-1" green, roundish	yellow flowers in spring, red berries	Berberis wilsonae, showy salmon-red berries, good screen
18	Barberry, Wintergreen	E dm-	hf-	6'/6' m	dense, upright, d. green, thorny	3" thorny, d.green, leathery	red to pink flowers, blue-black berries	Berberis julianae, thorny barrier, red fall color, burns in cold
19	Camellia, Japanese	E -m-	-fs	15'/8' m	d. green, open, upright, some tree-like	d. green, glossy, oblong	red to pink & varies with variety	Camellia japonica, many varieties, need drained, slightly acid soil
20	Camellia, Sasanqua	E -m-	hf-	12'/7' m	d. green, open, some like small tree	2" dark green, oblong	red to pink flowers in fall & winter	Camellia sasanqua, will take sun in good, drained & slightly acid soil
21	Cotoneaster, Franchet	E dm-	hf-	10'/10' m	l. green, gray, arching mound, open, irregular	1 1/2" gray-green oval, red in fall	orange berries	Cotoneaster franchetii, dry area plant, banks, loose screen
22	Cotoneaster, Parney	E dm-	hf-	8'/8' m	gray-green, arching mound, open, irregular	2" gray-green, oval	red berries, long lasting	Cotoneaster parneyi, bank cover, dry areas, loose screen
23	Euonymus, Evergreen	E dm-	hf-	10'/8' m	d. green, dense, upright, irregular	2" d. green, oval, gloss		Euonymus japonica, hardy, sun, good drainage or mildew, neat varieties
24	Euonymus, Winged	D dm-	hf-	10'/15' m	twiggy, dense branching, flat top, d. green	d. green, rose fall color	inconspicuous flowers, orange-red fruits	Euonymus alata, neat varieties background, corky branches
25	Fiberlily, New Zealand	E dm-	hf-	6'/6' m	green, bunch of upward sword leaves	long, narrow, l. gr. sword leaves	red-brown flower stalks, yellowish fl.	Phormium tenax, neat varieties with bronze & variegated leaves, accent

COMMON NAME	SOIL (m ev.green or / D deciduous / d dry / 3 moist / x wet)	SUN (3 hot / - filtered / s shade)	SIZE (height / width / growth rate: 1 slow / 3 medium or / f fast)	APPEARANCE	LEAF	FLOWER BERRY BARK	OTHER INFORMATION Botanical Name
26) Forsythia, Border	D	dm-	hf- 10'/10' m	arching, irregular, open, green	1" elongated, green	yellow flowers in Feb-April	Forsythia intermedia, nice showy early bloomer, mix with evergreens
27) Forsythia, Greenstem	D	hf-	10'/10' m	stiff-looking, olive green stems, green, irregular	1" elongated, green	yellow flowers in Feb-April	Forsythia viridissima, showy, blend with evergreens, not showy out of bloom — same for all Forsythias
28) Forsythia, Weeping	D	dm-	hf- 8'/8' m	drooping branches, irregular, green	1" elongated, green	yellow flowers in Feb-April	Forsythia suspensa, showy, needs to be blended with evergreens
29) Holly, Burford Chinese	E	dm-	hf- 8'/8' m	dense, d. green, holly-like, others rounded	2" d.gr., some holly-like, summer	nice red berries, summer	Ilex crenata 'Burfordii', protect from hot sun, screen, barrier
30) Holly, English	E	dm-	hf- 30'/20' s	dense, d. green, upright mound, prickly	2" with sharp points, d-green, gloss	red berries in summer, male plants = no berries	Ilex aquifolium, protect from hot sun, many varieties available
31) Huckleberry, Evergreen	E	dm-	hfs 8'/8' m	round, d. green, dense mound, open in the shade	1/2" d. green, oval, leathery	white flowers in March, dark edible berries	Vaccinum ovatum, native to Northwest, best in shade, forestry
32) Juniper, Blue Column Chinese	E	dm-	hf- 15'/3' m	regular, tall, narrow, blue-green, pointed, column	blue-green needles		Juniperus chinensis 'Columnaris' striking form, formal design
33) Juniper, Hetz Blue	E	dm-	hf- 15'/15' m	huge blue-green branches that shoot out at 45 degrees for 15'+	blue-green needles		Juniperus chinensis 'Hetzii', striking appearance, accent in large garden
34) Juniper, Hollywood or Torulosa	E	dm-	hf- 15'/5' m	green, upright, spiral, open branches	green needles		Juniperus chinensis 'Torulosa' neat accent plant, screen
35) Juniper, Irish	E	dm-	hf- 20'/2' m	d. green narrow, upright column	green needles		Juniperus chinensis 'Stricta', neat accent plant, use with high wall
36) Juniper, Meyer	E	dm-	hf- 12'/7' m	upright, blue-green vase, prickly	blue-gray-green needles		Juniperus squamata meyeri, good desert barrier, use carefully
37) (Laurel) – English Laurel Cherry	E	dm-	hf- 20'/20' m	green, mound, dense, can be tree-like	5" oblong, gloss gr., end rounded	summer black berries, white spring flowers	Prunus laurocerasus, part sun in hot areas, screen, hedge, tree
38) Laurel, Portugal	E	-m-	hf- 20'/20' m	d. green, dense mound, can be tree-like	2" oblong, gloss, rough edges		Prunus lusitanica, nice dense screen or dark background, or use as tree
39) Lilac, Common	D	-m-	hf- 20'/20' m	upright, green, open tree-like	4" oval, pointed, rough edges	pink to lavender in May	Syringa vulgaris, nice flowers, dry out plant in Aug. or will decline
40) Lilac, Persian	D	-m-	hf- 6'/6' m	upright, green, open, tree-like, arching	2" gr. leaves, oval, pointed	pale violet in May	Syringa persica, small plant, must dry out in Aug. or will decline
41) Mahonia, Leatherleaf	E	-m-	--s 10'/5' m	upright, umbrella-like, green leaves hang out from top	5" leathery, lobes with points (shallow lobes)	spring flowers	Mahonia bealei, plant in rich soil, touchy, neat accent plant, unusual
42) Mahonia, Lomar	E	-m-	--s 7'/5' m	upright, umbrella, green, leaflets that fan out from the top	leaflets, 12+, holly-like leaves	winter yellow flowers	Mahonia lomariifolia, accent plant, needs good soil, courtyards
43) (Mahonia)Oregongra Oregongrape	E	dm-	hf- 10'/5' m	upright, straight limbs, d. green foliage, prickly leaves	3" holly-like leaf, thinner, dark green	yellow clusters in summer	Mahonia aquifolium, native to Northwest, nice arid plant, screen, hardy
44) Madrone, Strawberry	E		hf- 20'/20' s	tree-like eventually, twisted limbs, green, reddish bark	3" oblong leaves, dark green	whitish flowers in fall-winter, red fruit	Arbutus unedo, grow as a tree or shrub, part sun in hot areas
45) Osmanthus, Delavayi	E	-m-	-fs 6'/7' s	d. green, prickly bush, arching limbs	1" round, holly-like, rough edges	white profuse clusters in March-May	Osmanthus delavayi, dense screen, dark background
46) Osmanthus, Fortunei	E	-m-	-fs 15'/10' s	prickly, dense, bush, d. green	4" holly-like, oval	white fragrant flowers in spring-summer	Osmanthus fortunei, screen, barrier, background plant
47) Osmanthus, Holly-Leaf	E	-m-	-fs 15'/5' s	dense, prickly, upright column, d. green	2" holly-like, dark green	fragrant white in fall-winter-spring	Osmanthus heterophyllus 'Illicifolius', screen, dark background

COMMON NAME	SOIL (E/D)	SOIL	SUN	SIZE	APPEARANCE	LEAF	FLOWER BERRY BARK	OTHER INFORMATION (Botanical Name)
Legend	m ev green / D deciduous	d dry / m moist / w wet	h hot / – filtered / s shade	height / width; growth rate: s slow / m medium / f fast				
48) Photinia, Chinese	E	dm–	hf–	35'/20' m	upright, reddish-green shrub or tree, dense, rounded	8" green, rough edges, elongated, rounded end	profuse white clusters April-May	Photinia serrulata, nice shrub or tree, feature plant or screen, mildews
49) Photinia, Fraser	E	dm–	hf–	20'/20' f	a regular mound, dense, reddish-green, can be a tree	2" oblong, glossy new red growth		Photinia fraseri, nice screen or prune to a tree, fast growth, adaptable
50) Pampas Grass	E	dmw	hf–	10'/10' f	upright, narrow sword leaves from the ground, l. green	narrow 5' leaves razor edge, green	tall plume in summer white or pink	Cortaderia selloana, accent plant, barrier, hardy,
51) Podocarpus or Yew Pine	E	–m–	–fs	40'/20' s	upright, narrow tree-bush, green & lacey texture	4" long narrow, rich gr., gloss		Podocarpus macrophyllus, accent plant, shelter it, courtyards, tubs
52) Pieris, Chinese	E	–m–	–fs	9'/7' m	green, compacted, rounded, upright shoots, red new growth	2" red new growth, gr. oblong, pointed	white, drooping clusters in summer	Pieris forrestii, needs more shade, nice lush garden plant
53) Pieris, Japanese or Lily of the Valley	E	–m–	–fs	9'/7' m	upright, green, tiered growth dense	3" elongated, glossy, red new growth	white dangly flowers in summer	Pieris japonica, protect from hot sun or wind, nice lush garden plant
54) Pine, Swiss Mountain	E	dm–	hf–	20'/15' s	upright, multi-trunked, d. green, pine	2" d. green, needles	inconspicuous cones	Pinus mugo, often confused with Mugho Pine, screen or dark backgr.
55) Privet, California	E/D	dm–	–fs	15'/12 f	dense, d. green, mounded shrub	2" oval, gloss, dark green		Ligustrum ovalifolium, hedge, greedy roots, variegated form
56) Privet, Common	D	dm–	hf–	15'/12' m	l. green, rounded shrub	2" oval, semi-gloss, l. green		Ligustrum vulgare, common hedge, greedy roots, smaller variety
57) Privet, Glossy	E	dm–	hf–	35'/20' m	d. green, tree-like, round-headed	5" tapering point gr. to dark, gloss	feathery flowers in August	Ligustrum lucidum, tree or shrub, street tree or screen
58) Privet, Waxleaf or Japanese	E	dm–	hf–	10'/8' m	d. green, dense, roundish, shrub	3" d. green, spongy, gloss, oval	white clusters in mid-July	Ligustrum japonicum, nice screen or small tree, shaped easily
59) Pyracantha (Scarlet Firethorn)	E	dm–	hf–	10'/8' m	rounded bush, upright branches, green, thorny	green, oblong, pointed, rough edge	white profuse flowers Mar-April, red berries	Pyracantha coccinea berries last all winter, nice
60) Pyracantha (Laland Firethorn)	E	dm–	hf–	10'/8' m	rounded bush, upright branches, green, thorny	green, oblong, pointed, rough edge	white profuse flowers Mar-April orange berries	Pyracantha coccinea lalandi, nice long-lasting berries, barrier
61) Quince, Flowering	D	dm–	hf–	10'/8' m	upright, green-red twiggy, arching	3/4" oblong, rough edge, gr., semi-gloss	pink flowers in early spring	Chaenomeles laginaria, hardy, nice early flower, middleground
62) Rhododendron, 'A. Bedford'	E	–m–	–fs	7'/7'	green, rounded, open	4" oblong, green, rounded	lavender-blue in May	Rhododendron 'A.Bedford', nice lush garden plant, acid soil
63) Rhododendron, Alice	E	–m–	–fs	7'/7'	green, rounded, open		pink-rose in April & May	Rhododendron 'Alice', nice lush garden, early flowering, acid soil
64) Rhododendron, Coast	E	dm–	hfs	10'/10' m	green, open, rangy, tree-like	4" oblong, green, rounded	rose flowers in early summer	Rhododendron macrophyllum, neat in tree form, native to Pacific coast
65) Rhododendron, 'Cornubia'	E	–m–	–fs	7'/7'	green, open, rounded		red flowers in February-March	Rhododendron chryseum 'Cornubia' nice early bloomer, acid soil
66) Rhododendron, Falconeri	E	–m–	–fs	25'/20'	tree-like, coarse, green, open	9" leathery, reddish	blooms after 20 years	Rhododendron falconeri, neat for large gardens, acid soil
67) Rhododendron, Loderi	E	–m–	–fs	8'/8'	green, rounded, open	large medium green	white to pink in May	Rhododendron keiskei "Loderi', nice lush garden plant, acid soil
68) Rhododendron, 'Pink Pearl'	E	–m–	–fs	7'/7'	green, spreading	green	pink in May	Rhododendron penakonese "Pink Pearl', acid soil
69) Spiraea, Thunbergi	D	dms	hfs	5'/5' m	arching, mound, green, many limbs	reddish fall color	white in April	Spiraea thunbergii, adaptable, twiggy looking, nice flowers

COMMON NAME	ev green or deciduous	SOIL (d dry, m moist, w wet)	SUN (h hot, f filtered, s shade)	SIZE height/width	growth rate (slow, medium, fast)	APPEARANCE	LEAF	FLOWER BERRY BARK	OTHER INFORMATION (Botanical Name)
70) Spiraea, Vanhouttei	D	dms	hfs	6'/6'	m	arching mound, blue-green, many limbs, twiggy	soft, l.green, roundish 1"	white flowers in June-July	Spiraea vanhouttei adaptable, twiggy, nice flowers
71) Viburnum, Burkwood	D	dm-	hf-	12'/5'	m	d. green, dense shrub, ragged new growth	3" d. gr., hairy under, gloss	profuse white flowers in February-March	Viburnum burkwoodii, nice middle-ground, foresty filler
72) Viburnum, European Cranberry Bush	D	dm-	hf-	15'/15'	m	arching mound, green, twiggy, many stems arching up	4" maple-like gr. leaf, coarse	white, flowers in late May	Viburnum opulus, nice middle-ground filler, showy flowers
73) Viburnum, Leatherleaf	E	-m-	-fs	15'/5'	f	upright, d. green, coarse, shrub	8" oblong, d.gr. rough, fuzzy under	whitish flowers in spring	Viburnum rhytidophyllum, nice shady garden, background
74) Viburnum, Snowball	D	-m-	hf-	15'/15'	m	dark green, mound, twiggy	5" oval, d.gr., veined	white snowball flowers in May	Viburnum plicatum, nice showy flowers

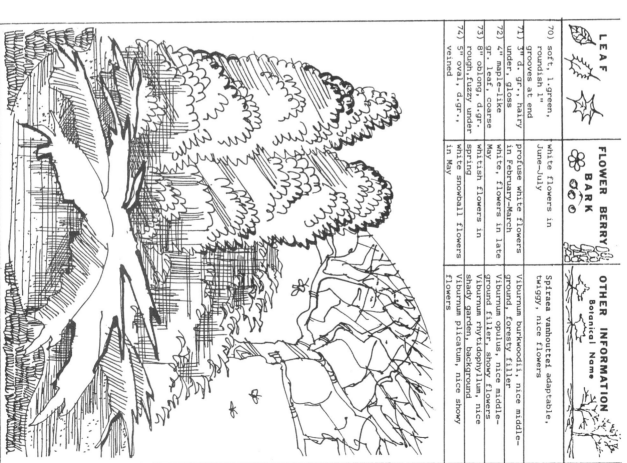

Conclusion:

Well, we have covered lots of information in this little book that begins with the basics of landscape design, and we discussed the importance of making good plans before launching off on a big "Pee Wee" type adventure. Paper is much cheaper to mess up, than your yard. The cost estimating process was described which is essential, since it takes a few bucks to purchase quality landscape materials. Some of the fundamental elements of planting design were described that combines the practical use of plants with the aesthetic use of plants. This part of the design is really important because the trees and shrubs dominate the finished grounds and continue to do so since they grow each year which tends to amplify good or bad design.

Once the planning process was described, this guide included the "down and dirty" part of landscaping that boils down to good ol' fashioned work! Yes, work. The factor that made America great, and this was the roll up the sleeves type work. If people despise work, then draw the plans and hire some hard working souls that can hack the rigors of landscaping. If you are into exercise then landscaping is equal to the health spa, and you reap an important fringe benefit such as a neat landscape. Just plan the project right, so you don't burn out in the middle of it and are forced to leave the yard a torn up, muddy mess that just sits there begging for completion. This can cause guilt, anxiety, and finally depression which no one needs, since our world is full of these horrible viles. I don't mean to drift in psychology, but somewhere out there everything connects in this grand mystery that we are all caught up in. Well, anyway back to the work. Plan the labor carefully with equipment rental, the weather, and your time, to avoid what is known in the trade industry as 'screw ups.' Follow the steps of weed clearing, soil preparation, grading, drainage, irrigation, planting, weed control, lawn planting, and maintenance then everything will be cool!

The irrigation section touched on the essentials of sprinkler design for the typical, uncomplicated yard. This section may require several readings since irrigation appears to be overly technical, but most people can figure the simple yard system out. Just get the magic number right, pick out good heads, space the heads right, and study the pipe sizing routine. Lay out the zones, locate the valves, and install the doublecheck valve after the water meter. Now, hook up the timer, kick back with a beer and enjoy the steamy jungle that you created with your own two hands.

Finally the plant charts will be valuable in selecting the right plants for most situations. The lists have all the important information such as soil, sun, size, growth rate, common name, botanical name, and the appearance of the plant.

Well good landscaping and if you have any comments write, and future editions will include reader comments.

THE END OR
THE BEGINNING

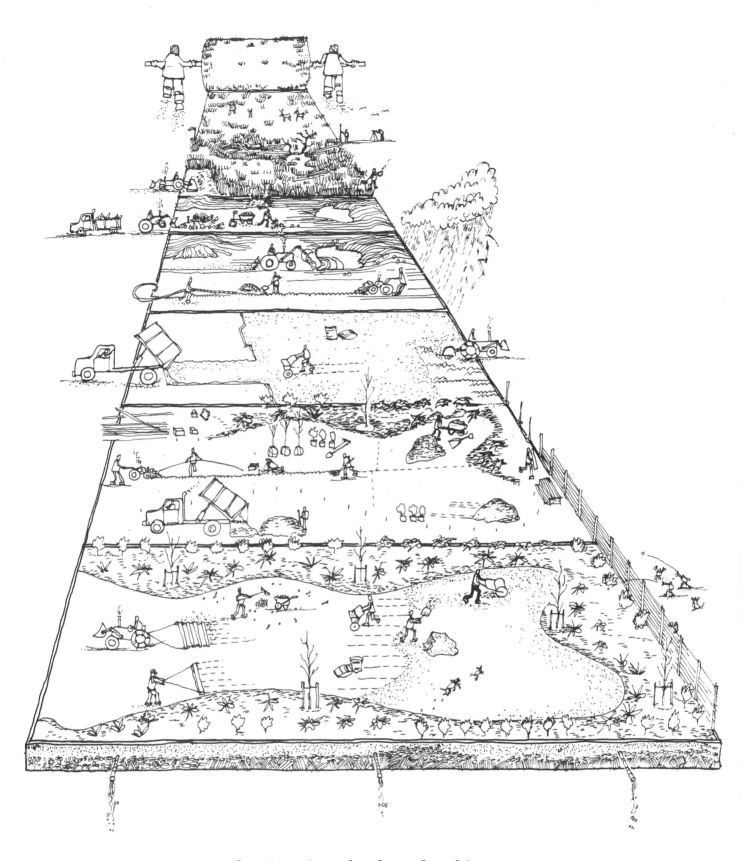

One picture is worth a thousand words!